Potholes, & Padlocks, & Poverty

Unlocking the Mystery of Global Missions

STEVEN M. KUHN

Guardian BOOKS

Belleville, Ontario, Canada

POTHOLES, PADLOCKS & POVERTY
Copyright © 2007, Steven M. Kuhn

Scripture taken from the HOLY BIBLE, NEW INTERNATIONAL VERSION ®. Copyright © 1973, 1978, 1984 by International Bible Society. Used by permission of Zondervan Publishing House. All rights reserved.

Library and Archives Canada Cataloguing in Publication

Kuhn, Steven M., 1978-
    Potholes, padlocks & poverty / Steven M. Kuhn.

ISBN 978-1-55452-208-8 (pbk.).--ISBN 978-1-55452-209-5 (LSI ed.)

    1. Kuhn, Steven M., 1978- 2. Missions--Mozambique.
3. Missionaries--Mozambique--Biography. 4. Missionaries--Canada--
Biography. I. Title.

BV3625.M66K84 2007   266'.023710679   C2007-904783-1

**For more information or
to order additional copies, please contact:**

Steven Kuhn
Email: steve@stevenmkuhn.com
Web: www.stevenmkuhn.com

Guardian Books is an imprint of *Essence Publishing,* a Christian Book Publisher dedicated to furthering the work of Christ through the written word. For more information, contact:
20 Hanna Court, Belleville, Ontario, Canada K8P 5J2
Phone: 1-800-238-6376 • Fax: (613) 962-3055
E-mail: info@essence-publishing.com
Web site: www.essence-publishing.com

Table of Contents

Acknowledgement

This project started as a bit of an accident: hearing about our upcoming mission trip to Mozambique, Africa, two people who have never met made the same suggestion to us in the same week: "You should make a blog." Laura and I had a simple response: "What is a blog?" But we researched it, and decided to start writing about our adventures. And along the way, people kept encouraging us to keep writing, to keep reflecting, to keep learning.

And then a strange thing happened. Countless people—friends and strangers alike—wrote to us to encourage us to publish our reflections. Really publish them; not just on the internet, but on paper, in a book that can be highlighted and written on, and get all dog-eared.

This project would not have happened were it not for the hundreds of people who supported our mission trip in a multitude of encouraging ways: financially, through prayer, and by reading early editions of this manuscript sent out over the internet as a constant reminder that we were alive and well. What a wonderful lifeline it was for us in Mozambique knowing that not a single day went by without at least one friend or family member signing onto the internet to read about what we had been experiencing.

This book is dedicated to the continued development of a program to strengthen the financial capacity and stewardship practices of the Palavra Viva Evangelical Church in Mozambique. It is dedicated to the continued development of the program's coordinators, Mario and Samuel, two Mozambicans who have a desire to change the direction of their country, and to Glenn Berryman, a friend and missionary whose number of references in the following pages does not accurately reflect the size or importance of his contribution. I pray that all three of these men are blessed with continued strength and success.

More than anyone, this book is dedicated to my lovely wife, Laura, who never ceases to encourage me, to pick me up, to correct me and check my facts. She never ceases to listen to my bold and crazy ideas, even if they are markedly different than the bold and crazy ideas that I shared with her just the day before. Without her, I would have been sitting at home in Canada this year and you would be checking the sports scores or the movie listings rather than reading this book. Thank you.

Steven M. Kuhn
Maputo, Mozambique
June 2007

Introduction

We have taken several walks through Maputo's once-beautiful, now-neglected botanical gardens. Its trees are twisted and mysterious, as if they cling tightly to long-forgotten secrets of Mozambique's past. They are enchanted trees. Massive, old trees.

On one of our walks, Laura and I stopped to look at one particularly strange tree on the western edge of the garden. Branches do not sweep out elegantly from its trunk in any efficient pattern, but instead twist here and turn there. Knot here, elbow there. It was ugly, unusual. And yet it was beautiful.

Straight lines are not natural. Like these trees, nature is full of twists and turns, full of inefficiencies, full of surprises. So too are social systems, so too a country's history, so too is our experience in Mozambique. Our world teaches efficiency, but God builds beauty through unusual patterns and unique paths. You will quickly notice through the pages of this book that our work and experiences in Mozambique are full of plot twists, like the gnarled old tree. And I hope that you will also see God's fingerprints all over the story. Sometimes the sudden and unexpected turns wake us to the reminder that God is in control; that He is the author of our story.

We must live in this world in order to fulfill the mandate of the Great Commission, but the Prince of Peace encourages us not to buy into the deception that this world has to offer. Black is not always black, and white is not always white. Poverty is not always conquered with cash, just as my best wisdom is not always wise. I came to Mozambique expecting that I would set up a small bank, lending money, transforming lives five or ten dollars at a time. But once I met these people whose lives were to be irreparably transformed by my beneficence, my eyes were opened to a reality that is much more complex—and much more hopeful—than the caricature of Africa that I had drawn in my mind.

That caricature has been replaced by a montage of full-colour photographs: of the smells of the city, of the people, of the warm air; it has been replaced by memories of friendships cultivated and blossoming. Memories of birds singing, children playing, dogs barking.

But these are my memories. Just as the gnarled tree twists unpredictably in three dimensions, the stories captured in the following pages reflect experiences of a given time and a given place. The clock can never be set back; the conditions and actors will never be the same. Our presence shaped the events that unfolded around us; you cannot have the same set of variables leading to the same set of outcomes. No two branches of the gnarled tree are the same.

Our journey does not start amongst the enchanted trees of Maputo's botanical gardens. It starts back at home, back in Canada. It starts in a spot both familiar and comfortable to us. It starts when God tapped us on the shoulder and whispered gently in our ears, "Come, follow me."

Fitting the Missionary Hat on Our Heads

We Will Follow

Laura and I have long dreamed about travelling for a year. The dreams started even before we were married. Maybe it would be nice to spend a year going to school in London or Paris, or working in Melbourne or Munich. We never dreamed that we would spend a year living in sub-Saharan Africa. Never, that is, until late last fall.

Planning and discussions have been in the works for many months, often behind closed doors, and now our departure is just two months away. Just two months until we set our careers on the back burner, sell our car, rent out our home and move to Maputo, Mozambique to volunteer alongside a US-based, Christian church-planting organization.

We are excited, yes, and more than a little nervous. We do not think of ourselves as the overly adventurous sort. Nor overly religious, though we do try to follow wherever God leads. We are not theologians or fanatics. We are normal. Average.

I have been invited to Mozambique to establish a micro-enterprise development program to help poor people create their own employment opportunities through training and small loans. That is a bit of a mouthful, and not much more than a cliché at this point. *Help people help themselves. Teach a man to fish....* A group of missionaries operating in Mozambique have focused on spiritual formation, but are coming to realize that the Bible's teachings ring hollow without basic physical needs being met as well. What the program will look like in practice is anybody's guess at this point.

My wife Laura will be teaching at the Christian Academy in Mozambique (CAM), a small Christian school of about 50 English speaking students from around the world. These are kids of missionaries, foreign diplomats and business people. Laura, who worked in Canada as a biomedical engineer conducting laboratory research, will be teaching math and science courses to high school students. Her job is a little easier to picture than mine, but she will not know exactly what classes the school's director needs her to teach until a couple of days before starting.

Laura would like more time to be prepared. I suspect that we are going to be wishing for "more time to be prepared" many times over the next year.

This will not be our first time in Africa. Two summers ago, we travelled to Mozambique as part of a team of seven Canadians from St. John United Church in Hamilton, where Laura's dad was then serving as the senior pastor. On that occasion, we were in Africa for about two weeks, and in Mozambique a grand total of four days. Maybe five. I can remember the day not so long ago when I gained enough knowledge about Mozambique to be able to point it out on a map. We will be forced to step out of our comfort zones this year.

We spent much of those days two summers ago in Khongolote, a sort of red-mud-paved suburb of Mozambique's capital city, Maputo, working alongside Mozambicans to build a cement block church building to replace a large canvas tent that they had been using for worship. We learned through this process that construction in Mozambique is an activity done by hand: in order to build a wall, we started by mixing cement and casting blocks in a mould, lining them up under the heat of the African sun to dry before setting them in place. Prior to the tent, the church's first home, shortly after the community was relocated here as a result of severe flooding five years ago, was the shade of a tree on the same site. That seems like a huge leap of progress in a few short years.

This brief exposure to Maputo is helping us to be a little more excited—and a little less nervous—than we would otherwise have been for the coming year. But we are also keenly aware that our view of Africa will not be the sheltered, romanticized view of constantly upward progress that we acquired on our first visit. The story of Africa is not all one of trees-to-tents-to-cement-block-shelters. We will be challenged in the year ahead to live on the edge of stress and discomfort. That is where people allow God to do His best work.

Displaced

The first step towards entering a new culture is taking one step out of the familiar one.

In anticipation of having our townhouse rented before leaving Canada (which has not happened yet), we have packed up our belongings and put them in storage in Laura's parents' basement. Packing up and storing our stuff was a major undertaking—and one that sobers us to the reality of just how much stuff can accumulate over time. Anyone who has moved recently can empathize with us, I am sure.

Of course, we are not complaining. In Mozambique, as in many parts of the world, people would welcome our problem of having sore muscles because of having to haul so many belongings. Instead, their problems are much more fundamental.

Many do not worry about whether or not their stainless steel bread basket matches the decorative theme of the kitchen. Many are too busy worrying about where to get the bread to stick in the only basket that they have.

Renting our townhouse is a critical step in our journey: since we have now both left our jobs, we are not receiving any income, but strangely enough the bank is still insisting that we continue with our mortgage payments every month. Our empty house is a good reminder that our journey is about to begin; the fact that it is not rented yet a reminder that the road ahead will not always be smooth.

We are now homeless, and will be for the next two months, until we finally get to move into our apartment in Maputo at the beginning of September. In the meantime, we will be moving around a lot and living out of suitcases. Already we cannot find some of the things we need. I know I packed that somewhere.... What a relief it will be in September when we have a home of our own, and can unpack these bags!

A Taste of What's Ahead

Laura and I woke up this morning early enough to wake the roosters—3:20am. Laura's dad drove us to the airport in time to catch a 6:20am flight to Indianapolis, where we will spend our first couple of weeks participating in a cross-cultural training workshop before heading to Africa.

We had naively assumed that we would have a couple of weeks' reprieve before having to stare down a foreign culture. That was before lunch.

We were in the Dulles airport, Washington DC, when the hunger pangs of lunch started to tug at us. We ordered our favourite sandwich at the Subway fast-food restaurant: a 12-inch chipotle southwest steak and cheese. We like to order one big sandwich and split it.

As Subway's "sandwich artists" were busy preparing our subs, I commented to Laura on the dual wonders of globalization and standardization: there we were, standing in a foreign country, ordering a familiar sandwich that was being prepared by hands trained with a common set of standard operating procedures. Our sandwich would taste exactly like it would were we back home in Canada. Or so I thought.

"What kind of sauce would you like, Ma'am?" the Artist asked, as he was trained.

"Chipotle sauce," Laura replied, "and some sub sauce, too."

Sub sauce. The staple sauce that is put on virtually every sub in Canada. So ubiquitous that the mysterious liquid is called just that. Sub sauce.

The Artist dropped the toppings in his hand and stared, and his colleague followed his lead. I felt as though we had uttered some *verboten* phrase, like French fries after 9/11. Apparently the Americans are not familiar with sub sauce.

They had no idea what we were asking for.

Of the selections that they offered, we opted for some oil and vinegar, but it just was not the same. We are only in the United States, one or two steps across the longest undefended border in the world, and already we have taken baby steps away from familiarity. But culture shock is bound to get worse than this.

America's Africans

This morning, still in Indianapolis, Laura and I decided that we would attend a Missionary Baptist church. We did not know anything about Missionary Baptists, except that its adherents are predominantly African American. Visiting them seemed like as good training as any for our immersion into Mozambique.

Our first option was Mount Moriah Missionary Baptist Church. It took us about 30 minutes to get to approximately the right area of town, and another 30 minutes to realize that we could not find the mystery address. For all we knew, we were not even in the right area of town.

Potholes, Padlocks and Poverty

Those last 30 minutes of driving around opened our eyes to a lot of poverty in the United States—especially in the neighbourhoods where African American churches are located. Either we do not know the same breadth and depth of poverty in Canada or, at least, it is more hidden in the high-rise complexes of public housing. Or maybe just hidden behind the tinted glass of our car windows as we drive to suburbia.

Our second option was Greater Prince of Peace Missionary Baptist Church. It was a bit easier to find—we found it about 20 minutes away from the neighbourhood where Mount Moriah was not, though the two neighbourhoods were similar: very narrow paved streets without curbs; old and poorly maintained housing with wood siding, often unpainted. Broken windows. Rusted cars.

We arrived five minutes after the time posted on the wooden sign on the lawn, but were still the third and fourth people to arrive. We were greeted warmly at the door by some folks assigned to do so, and again inside by "Sister Johnson," a lovely lady with a 17-month-old little girl in tow. The leaders had us singing before the pianist arrived, and reading scripture before the preacher arrived. By 30 minutes into the service, most people had walked through the door, perhaps 40 in all; all were African American.

We would have liked to take a picture inside the tiny church, but were sensitive to the worshippers whose lives we were entering; we wanted to be received as participants, not as tourists visiting a living, breathing museum display. We were conspicuous enough by our whiteness.

The choir was very loud and enthusiastic—think *Sister Act*—though the tuning was not perfect and the first soloist sharp and nasal. But we did not mind—the last time we heard singing like that was at the Khongolote church outside of Maputo, Mozambique! It is fascinating to see African culture in the United States, realizing that these are not the sons and daughters of immigrants, but of people kidnapped out of their villages for the slave trade hundreds of years ago. Some of the people in this room may even have come from Mozambique.

The congregation did not share the choir's passion. A few people clapped; some called out in response to the preacher. Most sat relatively still and listened. The choirs often receive the attention, but those bodies in the pews are real as well. The preacher's message, though it lasted 30 minutes, was a simple, one-point thesis using heart language. He spoke of "expecting the unexpected," and talked about how everyone has fallen on hard times at one time or another—like having the electricity cut off, or receiving an eviction notice. He said that those of us who have not just need to keep living, and we will. Everybody could relate. Everybody said amen.

Despite the readily apparent poverty of the congregation, an offering was collected three times: once for "mission" (probably inner-city work), once for the general fund and a building fund, and a third time as a gift to the guest preacher. The men were also reminded of their $10 per month "obligation," and the entire congregation was reminded several times of the $25 "requirement" for the pastor's anniversary fund. Their poverty certainly did not restrain their sense of generosity or duty to the work of God.

The church finally let out at 1:35pm—two and a half hours after its scheduled starting time. The congregants had to rush home for lunch: evening worship was scheduled to start at 3:30pm. Welcome to Africa in America.

Professional Volunteers

The organization with which we are working considers itself a "faith-based" organization. What they mean in plain language is that nobody draws a salary—imagine the low overhead costs! Each employee—of which there are over 200 in several dozen countries around the world, plus another 30 or 40 at headquarters—is responsible for raising his or her own salary through donations. This applies to everyone from the president to the mailroom clerks. Imagine your employer approaching you and asking that, in addition to all of your job responsibilities, you are also required to knock on doors asking people to donate your salary year in and year out.

On a visit to his house, I asked the president how he motivates and directs employees, given that their paycheques do not come from their employer. He told me that he and his board of directors must treat the organization's employees as if they were volunteers. Imagine the dilemma that he would face if he were required to dismiss an employee for underperformance, since recruiting replacements is so challenging; an employee performing half his duties is better than the position sitting vacant for the months or years required to recruit someone willing to fundraise their own salary.

The night after our visit with the president, we were invited to dinner with an employee, so I asked him his thoughts about needing to raise his own money. He understood why I was questioning the strategy, but did not mind it himself. Formerly a sales executive with a Fortune 500 company, he came to the organization with a sales background, so he was used to asking people for money. And used to being rejected.

Most employees accept this as a way of life; as we have discovered, it is not uncommon for people to spend their entire career with this same organization. On the other hand, Laura and I know of several people who have resigned in recent months, unable to find enough people to contribute towards their living expenses year in and year out.

Preparing to embark on this strange new frontier of volunteering-as-occupation, Laura and I spent our spare time across several months making presentations to large groups and small, hosting fundraising events and writing many letters, all with the hope of capturing the imaginations of people who are willing to contribute to missions and development work with their money.

And people have responded!

In fact, some of the people that we talk to are only too pleased to give money, seeing it as a way to relieve any sense of obligation to actually travel to Africa themselves. It is perhaps the first time in my life that I have heard people express *relief* to be asked to provide financial support!

As we begin our work abroad, about 75 percent of our estimated budget for the year has been provided: over $30,000 from 100 different families. That is an absolutely amazing testament of support from a very broad range of people. And it is a wonderful encouragement from family, friends and some perfect strangers as we set off to tame the wilds of Africa.

Old Wounds

Yesterday, a group of terrorists from Kashmir detonated eight bombs on the public transit system in Mumbai, India, killing over 200 people.

This morning, Israel stepped up its offensive against its neighbours by attacking Lebanon in response to the kidnapping of two Israeli soldiers.

Earlier in the week, Japan was rumoured to be considering "pre-emptive strikes" against military targets in North Korea in response to the latter's missile-testing program.

We have been reminded three times this week that the world is a violent place.

Mozambique is no stranger to violence. As a colony of Portugal for many centuries until 1974, Mozambique suffered the violence of an independence struggle against a country that offered little more than neglect and abandonment. They were, it seemed to many, engaged in the most ironic of battles: fighting for independence from a captor that did not want them. The neglect was so apparent that many people were not even aware that they were living within a colony called Mozambique.

As is often the case, neglect is far worse than being left alone. Throughout centuries of colonial rule, Mozambique was plundered for its gold, its ivory, and—most devastatingly—its labour. In the nineteenth century, Mozambique's major contribution to international trade was its slaves, leaving it impoverished and depopulated. Many of those who were fortunate enough to not have been kidnapped and sold into slavery were *de facto* slaves of the state, forced to work in the mines of South Africa to fill the coffers of the Portuguese with gold. This is Mozambique's sad history of abuse, even before the nearly 30 years of war are taken into account.

I cannot recall whether or not Mozambique's years of war—which ended in 1992, including a post-independence civil struggle that echoed the Cold War geopolitics of the time—ever attracted the sort of international attention paid to some of the more infamous conflicts of the past half-century. It was certainly violent enough to warrant such attention: according to a report by the UN near the end of the conflict, 900,000 Mozambicans were killed, 3,000,000 were driven from their homes, and a further 8,000,000 faced starvation or severe food shortages—not throughout the 30-year period of conflict, but just during the eight-year period prior to the release of their report. The tragic reality is that, as in Rwanda, as in Darfur, as in too many countries, neighbour was encouraged to rise up against neighbour.

But for now this is all just numbers recorded in history books, albeit history books with slightly damp ink. I wonder what, if any, evidence of these old wounds we will witness when we finally arrive in Mozambique? Those wounds have had fewer than 15 years to heal. I am hoping to hear stories from those who have actually lived some of the more recent of the country's fascinating history to see glimpses of how it impacts their present lives.

A Lament for the "M" Word

Laura and I debated using the word *missionary* to describe our work. It is the shorthand that others use to describe the work that we are going to be doing, Laura reasoned. True, but it is also a loaded word that has been misused in the past and is politically charged in the present—particularly in the United States, where we have been staying these past few weeks. We have been finding that fitting the "missionary" hat on our heads is a bit of a tight squeeze.

It is difficult to be a Christian in a world that is too often dominated by conflict framed as "holy wars" between Christian and Muslim; the principle actors in these conflicts give both Christianity and Islam a bad name. But missionaries are not cultural crusaders bent on dominating the world. They are regular people. The new recruits preparing to be full-time, for-real missionaries include a grandfather going to Japan to serve as a maintenance worker for other missionaries, a young lady with a communications degree going to write promotional material for a Christian radio station in Haiti, and a young man with a gift for photography travelling the world alongside other missionaries to document their work.

The word *missionary* is used to describe all of this work because these people are motivated by their Christian faith to help others around the world. "Truly I tell you, whatever you did for one of the least of these brothers and sisters of mine, you did for me," Jesus says (Matthew 25:45).

Others have a difficult time squeezing into the missionary hat as well. The attrition rate for new full-time missionaries is very high; we have been told that up to 40 percent do not finish their first term. Some quit because of an emergency back home, an emerging health issue, or because of a lack of funding. The most frequent reason for which missionaries quit is that they could not get along with the other missionaries in the field. Missionaries' stress levels tend to be high as a result of working in a culture that is not their own, often in a language they do not know well, all without the close support of family and friends. This is the life that we have signed up for.

The week that we travel to Mozambique has finally arrived. Our journey begins tomorrow morning, with the plane's wheels lifting off the runway at 6:00am. We will reach our final destination—Maputo, Mozambique—the following morning. After 26 hours in transit, we will most likely need a nap.

Now, Unlock Your Own Mission Field

1. How far are you willing to go to answer God's call? What are the areas in your life that are off-limits to God?
2. What image do you have in your mind of missionaries? What stereotypes do you hold? Do you think that you could ever accept a call to missions? Why or why not?

Challenge Yourself:

Find a church in your community at which the predominant culture is different than your own. Attend a church service with them with your heart and mind open. Do not be critical; just experience it as they are experiencing it.

Eyes Wide Open

A Second Chance for a First Impression

We arrived in Mozambique yesterday afternoon after a relatively uneventful flight. We made it, and so did our baggage. Despite having been here before, some things are still surprising. Showering was our first order of business, but our hosts warned us that the water pressure in the shower was low. I had the first shower and, upon finishing, warned Laura to cut her already-low expectations in half. She was still surprised at the trickle that came out.

We also learned that there is no garbage collection. Instead, there are dumpsters out on the streets that get emptied on occasion, but that are often overflowing with trash. Despite garbage being everywhere, we were told of someone who is in jail for putting garbage in the dumpster outside of the appointed hours, though nobody seems to know when those appointed hours are. Maybe that is why so many people seem to put their garbage around the dumpster instead of inside it.

And speaking of government services, there is no mail delivery, either. There is a post office box somewhere downtown, but we have been warned that nothing of value should be shipped. Who knows what the threshold of value is in such an impoverished country—one man we met has had boxes of chocolates disappear.

The exchange rate has turned us into instant millionaire missionaries. With one dollar trading at about 25,000 meticais, even the poorest people in Mozambique can be millionaires. On our first Sunday, I gave 1,500 meticais as offering to a local church and only later realized my lack of generosity. In the fog of jetlag, giving 1,500 of anything struck me as being sufficient.

We will be staying with a couple of different families before getting our own apartment in September. We are glad to have such gracious hosts helping us navigate this new culture. Tomorrow morning's adventure will be going to a government office to apply for a resident visa so that we can stay longer than 30 days—and, perhaps more importantly, so that we can leave without risk of not being let back in the country. It is all made more challenging since we do not understand a word people are saying to us.

Caution: Risk of Drowning

If you have ever spent time volunteering for something, you will understand that feeling of getting in over your head—not because you cannot handle the job for which you volunteered, but because once you have volunteered for one thing, you will be asked to do more and more and more....

Today, Glenn and Kris (our hosts) took us to the school where Laura will be teaching so that she could speak with the school's director, get her schedule and books, and start preparing for the school year that begins in less than a week.

What she found out is that she has been asked to teach eight full-year classes. The school director piled her high with textbooks, workbooks, problem books, and other various who-knows-what books that Laura will sort through over the coming days. She is feeling a little overwhelmed tonight, but reading "Rookie Teaching for Dummies" (which she found on Kris' bookshelf) is helping. (To be honest, I am not sure how helpful the book is, but it is proving to be a great stress reliever. Every page or two, Laura breaks out into laughter. Most recently was a section titled "Wacky Hall Passes," in which the author describes some of his favourites that he has used, including a six-foot-tall cardboard cut-out of Captain Picard that some poor kids had to schlep to the 'loo. Hopefully it was not an emergency!)

A week before starting, the school is still trying to plug up some teacher vacancies. While I was there with Laura today, they tried throwing some of those vacancies at me to see if they would stick. It was easy for me to say no to kindergarten. They were more serious about mid-level math and English classes, but that is really not my passion. I hope they are not too persistent—and if they are, they might just see some kid running down the hall in a few weeks from now with a six-foot-tall cardboard cut-out in tow. After all, I would at least have to make it fun.

At Least I Am Not Drooling

I have often been warned to watch out for the onset of culture shock, but even as I had travelled abroad previously, I have always understood it to be primarily an intellectual experience—a sort of "that is a weird way of doing things" inconvenience, like our lack of sub sauce in at the airport in Washington. Though I do not profess to know the depth and breadth of culture shock yet, I now understand it to be less about inconveniences and more a full frontal attack on one's sense of competence.

At home, we derive our confidence and comfort from a sense of competence—a sense that, if I want to do something, I have the ability to go and do it—and the independence that flows from that competence. In a new culture, that sense of competence quickly fades.

At home, I was a fully functioning, independent adult. By contrast, in Mozambique I have the competence of a young child. In the past couple of days, I have needed assistance from my new friend Glenn to speak with a store clerk to purchase my own groceries, cell phone, (fill in the blank...). Even more so, I needed his help to navigate government bureaucracy to complete our resident permit applications.

Never mind the challenge of buying things. Just getting somewhere, anywhere, is taxing. I have borrowed a car but feel like a new driver in the right-hand-drive car on roads where obeying rules is the exception and potholes are the rule.

I have met several Mozambicans—Raul, Timóteo, Samuel, Juca, Ricardo—but I cannot move a conversation beyond basic pleasantries ("bon dia" and "obrigado") to get to know them, except with those who can speak broken English with me. I am even challenged by solitary activities, like recharging our laptop batteries, which requires some sort of adapter to plug a North American plug into a Mozambican wall (I looked at home, but could not find an electronics store that carries Canadian-Mozambican electricity adapters).

Worst of all, and perhaps punctuating my newly perceived lack of competence that marks the onset of culture shock, is that my days are not yet full, and I have not even completely mapped out a game plan for the next year. Laura is at school right now in teacher training, where she probably has too much to do, and I am feeling guilty for not being busy mid-way through our first week on the ground.

The truth is that I have quite purposefully declined several requests of my time (including successfully turning down the opportunity to teach at school). I want to go slowly at first to make sure my time is targeted in the most effective direction, rather than filling up with good things that are not my passion. One chunk of my time will be devoted to language study. The past couple of days have reinforced the need for me to speak and understand a basic level of Portuguese, in order to be as effective as possible in helping

Mozambicans and to rebuild the competence necessary to ward away culture shock. The challenge of learning a new language is somewhat lessened by the realization that for most people here, Portuguese is a second language as well. Most Mozambicans first learned to speak a tribal language at home (*Shangaan* is popular in Maputo province), and only learned Portuguese as the "trade language" of Mozambique while in school. That experience makes them imperfect speakers and very patient and gracious teachers of language.

On Driving and Culture

In Mozambique, drivers drive on the wrong side of the road. I mean the left side. Of course, it is not uncommon to see a driver, impatient with the progress of traffic, turn on his hazard lights and actually drive down the lane of oncoming traffic.

Chapas, the local name given to the swarms of privately operated transit minibuses, are notorious for doing this. They will make a centre lane in traffic and flash their headlights, indicating to oncoming drivers that they had better get out of the way, because the chapa is not going to give an inch.

The chapas always win. The drivers rarely own their minibuses and abuse them accordingly. The Portuguese word *chapa* has a more general meaning as well: sheet of steel. And that seems to be the only requirement for registration as a minibus. Certainly having a windshield is not a requirement. Neither is having all four tires firmly bolted on. Nor having a working set of brakes. Forget about seatbelts, too. If they are all working, there may be eight of them. Certainly not enough for the fifteen or more sweaty people shoehorned inside.

Traffic becomes most interesting when the game becomes chapa-versus-chapa. Winner takes all. Chapas aggressively pursue passengers, competing against each other in a high-stakes, flying-steel match of leapfrog. The driver's helper opens and closes the door and provides extra eyes and ears on the road. He also shouts destinations and pounds on the chapa's rugged sides to hurry his driver along.

I recently watched a chapa up the ante to beat his competitors. Already overflowing with passengers bashing their heads on the roof with each bump, the chapa driver hopped the curb and raced down the sidewalk, splitting pedestrians like a combine harvester working a wheat field. His door helper had to run alongside to keep up; so too did a passenger desperately—for some unknown reason—wanting a ride.

In the end, the chapa driver was forced to concede defeat, retreating to the paved roadway behind the victor.

It is easy to think that riding a chapa requires an unnecessarily high degree of risk. Risk not worth its reward. But entering the streets of Maputo is a high-risk venture regardless of method: walkers, drivers, cyclists, transit riders. We are all at risk.

When I first sat behind the wheel of a car here, I did not understand what I was seeing. Driving on the other side of the road, traffic seemed to flow backwards. Red lights did not seem to matter much, and they were hard to interpret: sometimes they would flash yellow before green, sometimes after. Missing from the traffic lights are the familiar patterns and rhythms of home. Often, they do not even work, reducing intersections to life-threatening chaos.

Before understanding the rules and being able to decode the hidden order behind the chaos, driving was scary and stressful. "Just find a hole, and drive through it," was the advice that I received. There is barely a soul who will stop and let another driver through. Occasionally drivers will be honked at for "gridlocking" an intersection. They will almost always be honked at for not doing so.

I quickly got used to chapa drivers who would go around me

while I was stopped at a red light and drive straight through the intersection ahead. I could count on that happening every day. What really set me back was when a pickup truck full of impatient police officers did the same thing. There was no emergency, but neither was there oncoming traffic, so, apparently, no reason to stop.

I often run red lights, not because I am in a hurry but because I fear that not running the red light will result in the unsuspecting driver behind me to run into the back of my car. Up to half a dozen cars run the red light at each change. Green lights, by consequence, do not signal clear passage.

Traffic is often terribly backed up, often traceable back to poor or selfish decisions by drivers or pedestrians. But now that I am comfortable with it, driving is enjoyable. For the most part, other drivers rarely react in anger when I make a mistake, perhaps only because "mistakes" are so common. And some rules are innovative, such as extra-wide shoulders on highways so that slower drivers can pull off the road without inconvenience and allow faster drivers to pass.

It is easy to think that the roadways would run more smoothly if they would just adopt some of our rules from home. But whenever engaging new cultures, we must always strive to be quick to listen and slow to speak. On the roadways and in the culture, it has been useful for me to step back and understand the structure behind the chaos before rolling up my sleeves to try to "fix" things.

Reunited in Khongolote

Khongolote is best described as a suburb of Maputo. It is an area of very dry red clay that the government set aside to relocate victims of Mozambique's severe flooding in 2000. When it rains, it quickly becomes an area of very thick, goopy red muck. Its dirt roadways are lined with simple cement-block homes with tin roofs.

Potholes, Padlocks and Poverty

This past Sunday was an exciting day for us because it marked our return to the church in Khongolote that we helped to build two years ago. We can now claim the satisfaction of seeing it completed and in use, even if we cannot claim any satisfaction from the eye-popping salmon-pink colour that has been painted all over its walls.

The Khongolote church property provides space not only for Sunday services, but also for a preschool attended by over 100 children, and some other all-purpose meeting space. Many things in Africa could justify having the "all-purpose" label applied to them. This week, I have been using one of these all-purpose spaces to get quickly down to business, learning by doing. I have been working with several Mozambicans—Raul, Ricardo and Alfredo—to deliver a two-week-long micro-enterprise training program as a pilot project for a group of eighteen Mozambican micro-entrepreneurs. It is exciting to see that the church in Khongolote has provided the stage for these two weeks of training. I am very deliberately not doing the training myself, not wanting to cast the impression that I am full of knowledge and must work to fill their empty vessels with that knowledge.

As a development practitioner, Christian missionary, foreigner—whatever label is applied—the objective (in my view) should be to remain in the background and make oneself dispensable as quickly as possible. My role is as a mentor, a guide, an encourager, a facilitator—but only where absolutely necessary as an up-front leader.

The key to creating a program that is sustainable is to ensure that it is led from the outset by those it will benefit. The drawbacks of this approach, of course, are a bit of a loss of control over the ultimate direction of the program and perhaps an implementation that is slower than the breakneck speed that we are usually accustomed to. However, creating a program that is firmly in the grasp of Mozambicans will ensure that they buy into the concept, have the confidence and skills required to keep it going after we leave, and most importantly that they remain the masters of their own destiny.

My burden is to keep these values front and centre in my mind, since Laura and I are only staying for a year and we hope, in that year, to create some lasting change.

One of the ways to create lasting change is to build bridges rather than to create something from the ground up—to connect people within our churches with services that already exist in their communities rather than trying to provide those services ourselves. In this spirit, my colleague Glenn and I have been conversing with a local microcredit lending bank run by a large international charity about the possibility of providing business loans for this group of trainees. There is no need for us to reinvent the wheel at every turn and make mistake after mistake that others have already learned from. If micro-lending organizations already exist in Mozambique, we do not need to start another.

Similarly, when our micro-enterprise training program introduced informal savings and credit circles last week, the students were already familiar with the concept—they frequently implement them (called *xitiques* in Shangaan) to purchase their homes rather than using traditional bank mortgages (which are inaccessible to them).

To understand how a xitique (roughly pronounced she-teek) works, imagine this: a group of 20, 30, or 40 people meet weekly and each person contributes a small amount of money into a pot. Each week, a different member of the group brings the collected pot home and uses it for a planned major expenditure: perhaps the purchase of a house, or a large medical bill, or a child's tuition. By the time that everyone has received the pot, each person has contributed the value of their "loan" through their weekly contributions. It is a simple step to apply the already-familiar concept of a xitique to investment in an income-producing business—a step that many have already taken.

Once these two weeks of experimentation have been completed, Glenn and I will evaluate the successes and failures and will hopefully have inspired a couple of Mozambicans to start their own businesses in the process.

How the Other Half Lives

Before coming to Mozambique, I had heard the often-cited statistic that over half the world lives on less than two dollars a day, but as often as I have heard it, I have wondered what it really meant. The business training program that was offered in Khongolote this week has been a wonderfully instrumental accelerant in my quest to gain that very kind of insight.

On Wednesday, we encouraged the students to think about potential products or services that they could offer at their micro-businesses. In order to brainstorm product lists as a group, each student was asked to write down their three most recent purchases, and then together the class categorized the items into three groups: necessities, desires, and luxuries.

What a lesson in Mozambican culture! Their list of necessities included rice, bread, a candle, and fish. The class actively debated whether clothing and sandals were necessities or not—they eventually agreed that a basic level is necessary, just like in North America. Their desired items included cold drinks, sugar and tapioca.

Nobody in the class had purchased anything recently that was categorized as a luxury item, so the instructors asked the class to dream a list of luxuries. The list included a gas stove (which we will have once we move into our apartment, though there is a gas shortage in Mozambique right now, so it is a little unclear how useful it will be), a refrigerator, liver, salad dressing, and a computer. Nobody in the class had these things.

And nobody even dreamed of having a car, a boat, a cottage, or a vacation.

As an inducement to encourage attendance, I have been providing "breakfast" for the class all week—bread from a bakery two doors down from the church, so fresh that it is still warm. Fourteen loaves for less than two dollars. I also buy a can of jam, some butter, and tea. The number of meals people in Khongolote eat varies depending upon the amount of food that they have, but this simple breakfast late in the morning and a dinner late in the day is pretty typical, I am told, though sugar for the tea is somewhat special.

Graduation Day

On Friday morning we held a graduation ceremony for the eighteen participants of the micro-enterprise training program that has taken place over the past two weeks. It will take follow-up visits to all of these people in the coming weeks and months to really gain insight into the value of the program offered, but already I have seen some exciting fruit as participants' eyes were opened to simple business principles.

One lady shared during the post-training evaluation that the most important realization that she made during the two weeks of training was the need to separate personal and business finances. This lady shared how this simple realization will improve her business: before this training session, she did not know how much profit she was earning from the sale of charcoal, which is used for cooking. She put all of the money that she earned into her pocket, mixed with all of the money that she had on this Earth. She competed by offering the same product with the same terms of sale as her competitors. Now, knowing how much money she is making, she realizes that she can sell her charcoal for a lower price but insist that her clients pay right away rather than extending them credit. Under her old business model, her business was constrained because of a cash flow problem resulting from her receivables—that is, because people paid for her product up to a month after having purchased it, she would not have sufficient cash to purchase her next lot of inventory for the rest of that month. Now she knows that by insisting that her clients pay right away (and offering a lower price for doing so), she will improve her cash flow and be able to turn her inventory three times faster.

It is also exciting to see the participants and trainers actively challenging and debating one another with respect to business implementation and improvement. One of the most clear examples of this resulted from the bank credit lecture given by a representative from a local microcredit bank. The participants challenged the bank's business model and interest rates, and provided suggestions to one another about credit options that might be superior. Praise God that they are thinking critically about their options!

A Bump in the Road

Potholes are commonplace in the streets of Maputo. The bump that I hit today was more figurative, but no less frustrating. A few weeks ago, I was excited about the possibility of partnering with an already-established microcredit lending institution, leveraging its existing infrastructure and experience for maximum results. That was an early splash of excitement. And just a few days ago, I first started to realize that the splashed water was shockingly cold. I spent this morning exploring microcredit options that exist for poor entrepreneurs in Maputo. I did not expect to become so discouraged researching organizations that hold such promise.

There are three microcredit banks and more than twenty smaller micro-finance institutions officially registered with the government of Mozambique. There appears to be many options, but all three of the full-service "banks" offer similar loan terms: they require the lender to have a track record of success as demonstrated through an existing business, and they charge crippling rates of interest: for the smallest loans, the three charge between 5.5 and 6.5 percent *per month*. Business success is a lot more difficult to come by with such a high cost of capital.

(For the armchair economists in the group, you are right— developing nations do have higher interest rates than we would expect to have in a developed nation. But not that high. The Banco de Moçambique, Mozambique's central bank, reports that its overnight rate is just below 16 percent per annum, and inflation has been slightly negative for the past quarter.)

Microcredit is supposed to be a broadly accepted development tool. It is supposed to have freed poor entrepreneurs from the grips of money lenders and their usurious interest rates. 2005 was even declared the International Year of Microcredit by the United Nations and a cadre of other well-respected multinational organizations.

Why, then, are the poor still faced with such steep interest rates? And what requires large microcredit banks—operating as a registered charity in developed nations, receiving donations from well-intentioned Westerners—to charge such high rates of interest?

There must be a good explanation, but I have not heard it yet.

The potholes in Maputo are numerous and deep, but none yet deep enough to have swallowed my hope. Tomorrow we will start looking for alternatives.

Samuel, Micro-entrepreneur

Just how small does an enterprise need to be in order to be called "micro"?

Laura has been reminding me for days now (if truth be told, it has probably been two weeks) that I am in need of a haircut. What better opportunity than this to explore micro-enterprise in action and to get a glimpse into the life of a micro-entrepreneur.

Samuel is a young man I have gotten to know through his work as a guard at the house where Laura and I are staying for the next week and also as a guitar player at one of the local churches that we have attended a couple of times.

Samuel, who is in his mid-twenties, is a high-school student. Mozambicans are hungry for education. Many people missed out during the civil war that ended in the early 1990s and are now trying to catch up as adults.

Last week I learned that Samuel also owns a barber shop, so I asked if he would take me there some day. That day was today.

Samuel's shop is a small building made of *caniço* (pronounced "kan-ee-soo"), which is a thick, hard reed that is Mozambique's traditional construction material. The shop has a corrugated metal roof and a wooden door that is fastened closed with some stiff wire. Most days, Samuel has an employee who does the hair cutting. Today, however, Samuel would cut my hair because his employee did not show up for work.

The shop does not have electricity, so it closes at dark (which is about 6:00pm). The barber's main tool, a set of electric clippers, is powered by a car battery running through a transformer. The battery is recharged at a shop not too far away that has electricity. Each charge lasts nearly a week.

Samuel had never cut a white person's hair before. The trickiest part, he learned, was cutting the soft little hairs on the back of my neck. His blade was a little dull, but otherwise he did a great job.

Samuel has a price list posted on the wall. My cut cost 15,000 meticais, which is about 60 cents. Some fancier cuts cost up to 20,000 meticais. And yet, he manages to be profitable. When he set up shop a year and a half ago, he took out a loan of 5,000,000 meticais, which he was able to pay back in just a few months. On this day, he had a customer at the shop before me, and by the time I was done, there were several other people waiting their turn outside.

If you are ever in Maputo, I would definitely recommend Samuel's barber shop, though I would have to show you where it is since there is no sign out front (Samuel assured me that everyone knew it was a barber shop). And you just cannot beat the price.

NOW, UNLOCK YOUR OWN MISSION FIELD

1. Through what activities, skills, or relationships do you define yourself? What makes you valuable? How do you think God defines you?
2. Are you saying yes too often to too many things, leaving you feeling tired or burned out? Can you identify any things in your life—good things or bad—that are sapping your time or energy from doing that great thing that God is calling you to do?

Challenge Yourself:

Select one of the charitable causes that you support regularly and hear from its beneficiaries about how their lives are being transformed by your contribution. Learn to be a critical investor of your precious time and money.

Start with a Crawl, If Possible

Home, Sweet Home

Yesterday, for the first time in sixty-six days, Laura and I unpacked our suitcases. We are grateful for the hosts we have had over the past two months, but we are certainly glad to be able to relax in our own space for the remaining ten. We have moved into an apartment that is not too dissimilar to any apartment in any urban area back in Canada. As in any new home, we are still adjusting to some unusual sounds in the walls and smells emanating from the pipes. The electricity is a little unsteady, so the lights take a little while to come to life, and the water running from the taps is not potable, but those are minor inconveniences. There is a gas stove fed by a butane cylinder sitting on the floor beside it, which makes us feel a little like we are camping every time we strike a match to make something for dinner.

Africans need not maintain the same sharp distinction between "inside" and "outside" as we do in Canada, since the snow never flies here. On the balcony, there is both a laundry machine and a "water closet" in the truest sense of the term: the whole room serves as the shower stall, with the shower head positioned such that one could actually have a shower while sitting on the john, though I would imagine that doing so would result in the toilet paper being a little more soggy than I would like.

The most unsettling part about life in Maputo is the need for security. Our previous homes have been surrounded by walls or fences topped with razor wire. Those who cannot afford razor wire make do by cementing shards of glass from broken bottles onto the tops of their perimeter walls. Our previous homes have also had guards—not trained, uniformed soldiers carrying weapons, but boys whose job it is to open the gate when the *patrão* (boss) arrives and to provide a general presence around the house, for whatever that is worth. Here, our apartment lacks the soft comfort of razor wire, but is cocooned with metal grates over every possible opening. A heavy iron gate secured with two muscular padlocks is Mozambique's version of a screen door.

These features serve both to remind us of our need for heightened alertness and help us to feel safe at home. Most of the noise coming through our windows originates from the laughing mouths of children playing in neighbouring apartments. From in here, the reality of Africa seems very far away.

Searching for Balance

This morning I was given a preview copy of a report prepared by a Mennonite economic development association in partnership with the United Nations Development Programme. The two organizations studied the microcredit industry in Mozambique and concluded that the high interest rates that I have observed in my sampling of microcredit banks are indeed the market rates in Mozambique. They may be high, but they are what they are.

I arranged a meeting with a gentleman from a local microcredit bank to talk about their high rates and what, if anything, we could do to mitigate the underlying risks to bring the rates down for the specific borrowers that we have in mind. Maybe we could guarantee loans for selected individuals against our own pool of capital. Or maybe in partnership we could leverage their lending infrastructure to loan our own money at lower rates. The meeting was fruitless. He confirmed their high rates and indicated that they are likely to stay high for the foreseeable future, citing the need to generate a profit in spite of economic factors (high inflation, currency devaluation) and the high cost structure of running such an organization. Thinking about the roomy, plentiful office space and his silver BMW in the parking lot, I could not help but wonder if some of those costs were excessive. He also closed the door to any form of partnership, at least for now. Do not call us; we will call you, perhaps in a year's time. Or maybe longer.

In our churches are specific people who want to start specific businesses. Two men want to start the neighbourhood's first *papelaria*, a place where the community could come to make photocopies and type out official documents. A woman wants to start a bakery that specializes in cakes for celebrations. Traditional banks will not lend money to these people because they want to borrow too small an amount of money to be worthwhile and they have no physical collateral or dependable income to back a loan anyway. And now I have learned that the established microcredit community will not lend money to them since they are not borrowing money to capitalize an existing business. Even the microcredit lenders want to see a track record of success in business before putting their money on the line, which actually works out well since our potential borrowers balk at the microcredit banks' high interest rates anyway.

What can we do to help them? The first obvious answer is to reach into my pocket and lend them my own money at interest rates that are morally justifiable (a subjective test, to be sure). But there are problems with this approach. Many loans would not be repaid because I would not be willing to enforce them in the event of default. Am I prepared to take away a struggling business or a kitchen table from a poor African who is suffering financially enough that she cannot repay my tiny loan? Even if—especially if—I decided to lend my money with little hope of repayment, such a model is not sustainable. My money would quickly run out, as would any donations that I could pry from the hands of people back home. The program would not last long.

Until recently, I have been holding sustainability up as if it were the Holy Grail. Maybe it would be more valuable to simply help someone today. Maybe the objective should be to improve one life at a time and leave worrying about tomorrow for tomorrow. Loren Eiseley's "The Star Thrower" gracefully captures this thought:

> A young man was jogging down the beach one morning when he saw an old man ahead of him bend down, pick up a starfish and throw it into the sea.
>
> As he approached, the young man asked, "What are you doing?"
>
> The old man answered, "There was a storm last night that washed many starfish high up onto the beach. If I do not throw them back, the sun will kill them by noon."
>
> The young man laughed and said, "You are a foolish old man. The beach is miles long and there are thousands of starfish stranded on it. You cannot get to them all before the sun dries them out and kills them. What you are doing, old man, just does not matter."
>
> The old man picked up another starfish and threw it into the safety of the waves. "It mattered to that one!" he replied.

This old guy's approach is not sustainable. It is not helping the starfish to help themselves, and it cannot easily be scaled up to help all of the starfish, but it is helping a few of them through their immediate crisis.

My struggle is where to set the balance between immediate impact and sustainable improvement. Will providing Mozambicans with a source of income for today create a longer-term dependence? If I give a man a fish, he might become dependent on me for the next one. If I teach him to fish, on the other hand, he might starve trying to learn.

What is the right balance? My quest for an answer continues....

An Emergency Vacation

This weekend, Laura and I made a break for it. A run for the border. We had not planned on going to South Africa. Twenty-four hours before standing at the border, we were not even allowed to leave Mozambique because our resident visas had not been approved yet.

The emergency was that our (borrowed) car was having trouble. The only garage the owners trust is in Nelspruit, South Africa. It is not a completely comfortable feeling knowing that we had to drive 220 kilometres in a car whose state of repair was questionable, but even in need of repair, the 2000 Toyota Sprinter that we have borrowed is in the upper quartile of cars careening down the streets of Maputo. (The bottom quartile consists of cars that have either long since been abandoned at the side of the road or should have been.) On Wednesday morning, I went to the immigration office to see if our resident visas were approved. They were and—a near miracle, I am told—a week earlier than promised. We left on Thursday morning for Nelspruit.

South Africa was at once familiar and not familiar—comfortable and not. For the first time in weeks, strangers spoke English, but they did not understand our accent automatically. We still felt like foreigners, not completely able to let our guards down.

Our mechanic, an Afrikaaner named Ferdi, looked at our car Friday morning. It turned out that the awful screeching noise

41

that alerted us to trouble was caused by some metal something-or-other that was bent and rubbing against another something-or-other. Ferdi did not seem too sure himself but handled the repair personally and charged us 90 Rand (about $12) for his trouble. A small part of me would have felt a little more assured that our car was roadworthy again had he charged 900 Rand instead, like at home.

With the car's clean bill of health, Laura and I headed back to Mozambique. As the car brought us closer and closer to the border, an electrifying stress rolled through our bodies. Our chests tightened and our minds filled with dread. It was the first time that we realized that the emergency vacation was really for us, not the car. We only noticed the vice-like pressure of our adopted home when our escape to South Africa stopped the squeezing for a day.

In Trouble with the Law

We have been told that there are two things that are inevitable when driving in Mozambique: getting in an accident and, even more frequently, getting stopped by the police. And, inevitably, the latter just happened. Being stopped by the police in Mozambique, where corruption is commonplace, is a unique experience. For the most part, police officers in Mozambique are on foot. The police department has a few vehicles, but they are generally pick-up trucks with their backs filled with patrolmen, delivering police officers to their respective beats. The officers that stopped me today did so by waving at me from the side of the road.

They seemed so non-threatening that I pointed at myself ("who, me?"), and when they nodded I quickly considered which pedal to press. Stopping would be the right thing to do, but the officers are on foot, so what were they going to do? When the answer "shoot" popped into my head, I did what I would likely have done anyway: I pulled over and stopped.

The lead officer leaned down into my window and said something incomprehensible in Portuguese. I made an assumption, and pulled out my documentation. When he did not seem interested in it, I told him that eu não falo portuguêse. He could speak a little English.

He told me that he would follow me to the police station (when he walked around and tugged on my passenger door handle, I quickly realized that in his broken English, what he really meant to say is that he would sit beside me while I drove there.) His partner hopped in the back seat.

I later learned that I should not ever need to drive a police officer to the station.

After a few blocks, he told me that the fine for what I did was 2.5 million meticais, or about $100 dollars, which seemed steep for Mozambique, but in line with Canadian standards, and who am I to argue with the law anyway?

I later learned that such a fine is far too high.

We drove a couple of blocks, and then he said something again. I did not understand exactly, but something about "half." We could settle this without going to the station for half the fine. I knew that I only had about 300,000 meticais in my wallet, so I was not afraid to pull it out to show him. He was clearly disappointed. He was even more disappointed when I pulled out my empty pockets and assured him that there was not more hidden in the car either.

He discussed his options with his partner, took my money, and hopped out of the car. It was not long before I came to the realization that I had just paid my very first bribe to a government official in a developing country.

I later learned that the officers wearing green sweaters (as these gentlemen were) are pedestrian police and do not even have the authority to stop a car. Next time I will know better. I will still stop, even if I think they do not have the authority to pull me over. But next time, I will ask them for a receipt.

Homes and Cell Phones

I have been meeting with a young man named Mario twice a week to practice speaking Portuguese. I have been paying him for his services because it is truly been helpful and because, at 24 years of age, he is trying to finish school and look after his younger brother at the same time. He is looking for work as a translator at embassies, or as a chef. He loves to cook.

I met Mario at a local church that I attend more frequently than any other right now—perhaps once every second week. He took the initiative to approach me for a job and takes his commitment seriously.

Mario just showed me his new cell phone. It cost him $80, which I loaned him as an advance on his salary, to be paid back over two months. Cell phones are everywhere, and they are a major asset in Mozambique. Just yesterday I heard about someone who is in hospital suffering stab wounds from a screwdriver. The thief coveted her cell phone.

I am having a hard time believing that so many people can afford to pay so much money for cell phones. By contrast, Mario is also paying a mortgage of about $800 on the house he lives in. Because banks in Mozambique are not interested in such small loans (and may not consider his meagre structure to be suitable for a mortgage anyway), the home's previous owner holds the mortgage (and title to the house, until Mario has completed his payments). Mario pays whenever he can put together some savings. He is not expected to pay monthly.

In other words, I just lent him 10 percent of the value of his house to buy a telephone. I was shocked. Surely that is an obscene amount of money for a phone!

Laura and I dropped him off at his house recently, in a subdivision of Maputo called Polana Caniço. The clay brick house has three rooms, but it is only half built: only his bedroom is covered by a roof, which consists of corrugated steel sheets set across the tops of the walls. The walls are crumbling—poorly constructed, Mario says of the man he bought it from—and there are holes where windows might eventually go. And some common features of homes in Canada are unnecessary and unheard of here. You have a heater in your home? Everybody does? Most Mozambicans do not understand the Canadian climate and do not care to.

And other common features are luxurious, such as running water, which Mario does not have. He does not have electricity either, because he can neither afford to hook it up nor afford to pay the bills. It is all too easy to forget the luxury that we are enjoying in Maputo: our electricity costs about $40 a month, roughly the same as the monthly minimum wage.

Cell phones are as expensive here as they are in Canada, which make them exceedingly expensive for the average Mozambican. And yet nearly everyone has one.

Seeking Cultural Common Ground

In order to be as effective as possible in Mozambique, it is imperative that I develop a strong understanding of African culture. Spending time with people like Mario, who can help me to navigate the cultural rough waters is invaluable. With an open mind, I am trying not only to understand the culture of my adopted home but also am trying to understand how people within this culture interpret my own actions, shaped by my own culture.

How Africans treat money is particularly interesting and makes sense only within Africa's historical context. Many African cultures did not have any need for money until their colonizers came and required that they pay taxes to the colonial rulers. These taxes had to be paid in the colonial ruler's currency, requiring Mozambicans to take Portuguese jobs to earn Portuguese currency to pay Portuguese taxes. Mozambicans were no longer independent. As a result, money has historically been seen with a certain degree of contempt; it was introduced to extract power and resources from the continent's natural habitants.

It is obvious that, for various political and climactic reasons, Africa has endured severe poverty. By and large, Africans do not share Westerners' belief that they can live independent lives. Life is not a competitive race, but rather a cooperative, interdependent struggle. Survival requires the maintenance of a large safety net of family and friends. As one observer of African culture notes, "the ideal of unity in all things…[means that] being the richest man does not necessarily give status. Status is gained by willingness to share the riches with other people."[1] This cooperative spirit of African culture is founded upon the assumption of reciprocity— that I will help you with your need today because tomorrow it might be me who is in need. The Golden Rule.

Introducing Westerners into the equation creates tension on the system for one fundamental reason: the assumption of reciprocity breaks down. In the Westerner's eye, the African relent- lessly asks for more and more and more. In all likelihood, the African will never be in the position to repay our gifts because we will never be in need relative to them. Because of our wealth, the relationship is off-balance. We cannot be fully integrated into this culture without completely cutting ties to our financial and social networks in the West.

Africa's cooperative spirit has several additional consequences that further strain the relationship between Western and African culture. For instance:

---

[1] David Maranz, *African Friends and Money Matters*, p. 60.

- Africans believe that assets—money, tools, food—not being used are available for others to use. This makes sense within the African context: if there is not an excess of resources in general, then someone having more than needed means that someone else is in need. And they believe that the person in need has the right to take idle assets.

In fact, Africans believe that resources are to be used, not hoarded, and that hoarding is a selfish and unsocial act. Why keep for tomorrow what someone else needs today?

In the West, we have a deeply entrenched sense of individual property rights. What is mine is mine, and only becomes yours if I explicitly give (or sell) it to you. We tend to view Africans' reciprocity as tantamount to theft.

- As a counter measure to the above point, Africans often store their wealth in immoveable assets, such as Mario's partially built house, rather than liquid assets such as bank account balances that, somehow, are not unknown to neighbours.

To illustrate this point, one of my African colleagues, Raul, had been saving to get married, but was forced to postpone in part because his brother had a more urgent need for his savings. Now, Raul has accumulated just enough money to build one wall of a house for himself. To avoid his savings being taken again, he wants to build this wall now rather than waiting until he has enough money to build the entire house.

Mozambique is littered with partially built but already-occupied homes. In the West, we tend to view these piles of cement block and protruding rebar with a touch of contempt as the fruit of poor planning.

- More generally, sharing resources is the basis for many friendships in Africa, since doing so is vital to survival. By contrast,

Westerners tend to distrust relationships that are based upon (or even involve) the sharing of financial resources. A friendship based on money is no friendship at all, most of us would believe. He is not interested in being my friend, he is just after my money.

• Africans tend to be hospitable, sharing their resources spontaneously with those within their social sphere, but tend not to be charitable beyond their known world. Westerners tend to be charitable, sharing considerable wealth in a planned, anonymous fashion, often using large organizations as conduits for our generosity. We tend to be hospitable only to a point: meals are often shared amongst family and friends, but financial resources are only seldom shared within families and rarely with friends or neighbours.[2]

All of these points boil down into one irony-soaked understanding: Westerners living in Africa tend to look at Africans and interpret their constant requests for money and open-ended "borrowing" of assets as greedy and self-seeking; Africans looking at Westerners, meanwhile, see our very different cultural patterns—our constant planning and budgeting and our weariness of requests for money from friends—as being greedy and self-seeking as well.

Two very different approaches, viewed with the same suspicious interpretation by two very different groups.

Tangled in Red Tape

In African society, bureaucracy abounds. It is everywhere, not just in government. This realization percolated to the surface shortly after the intake line on our water heater sprung a leak,

---

[2] Thanks to David Maranz for verbalizing these African cultural traits.

squirting water onto the heater's electrical wire, resulting in some pretty decent fireworks—a little scary since our water heater is hanging from the wall in our bathroom. Naturally, I had to roll up my sleeves and do some plumbing work to sort the problem out.

I needed to ask for help from a friend. It took both of us, a hammer, and a set of vice grips to get the rusted, broken intake line off the wall, but that is just an aside. The real lesson in bureaucracy started at the hardware store, where I needed to buy a little adapter to fasten a new steel braided hose to the old water line.

Inside the hardware store, I was greeted by a man behind a counter. "Can I help you, please?" he said, or something like that. He spoke Portuguese. Knowing that I would have a hard enough time trying to describe this little plumbing gadget in English, let alone Portuguese, I came equipped with the old broken parts and asked for a pen and paper to draw a diagram.

"Oh, yes," the man understood what I was looking for. He quickly fetched one from the storehouse. Perfect, I said. So he took it away and wrote the name on a scrap of paper. Handing me the scrap, he directed me toward another counter.

Fewer than four paces away, I arrived at the second counter and handed the scrap of paper to a man waiting to receive me. He glanced at the paper, wrote the part number on another scrap of paper and pointed at a third counter. Six steps this time, crossing past the original counter.

The man at the third counter typed the part number into a computer and sent an invoice to a printer sitting beside a woman at a fourth counter. They were close enough that he could have handed her the slip of paper, but that is not the protocol.

I wish I were joking.

At the fourth counter, the lady asked me to pay. I realized that I did not even have the part yet, so I protested. Silly estrangeiro. Of course I do not have the part yet. Once I paid, I brought the invoice back to the man who first helped me, who went to the same shelves in the back to retrieve the same part that I needed, and got his supervisor to sign and stamp the invoice. Clutching my certificate of perseverance from the supervisor, I was now eligible to receive the part.

Four counters and six employees later, I shoved the $0.60 gizmo deep into my pocket, and headed for the door.

The plumbing adaptor fit perfectly, and screwed onto the pipe much easier than the old one had come off. But once the original leak was fixed, I was disappointed to find that the water shut-off valve had developed a steady drip.

I was not looking forward to having to replace the entire valve, so I found a small bucket to put under it and left it for another day. That evening, I casually mentioned the leak to someone who has been living in Mozambique for several years, and he told me not to worry about it—that in Mozambique, valves are "self-healing." A small smile and a pause. He then explained that pipes throughout the city are so corroded that within a week or so, the leak would rust shut. It would repair itself.

I laughed and hoped that it was true.

Today, three days after my plumbing work, the drip coming from the leaking valve has slowed nearly to a stop. I have no doubt that within the next couple of days it will have self-healed completely.

And now I have even more reason not to drink the tap water around here.

Fala português, por favor!

There are a lot of difficult things about engaging a new culture, but perhaps none as difficult and confidence-testing as learning a foreign language. Sometimes, like at the plumbing store, we can muddle through. But developing meaningful relationships with people demands a solid understanding of their language.

Laura and I have been working hard to learn Portuguese. For me, it is a part of my daily routine. In addition to spending two days a week conversing with Mario, I am also attending one-on-one classes three days a week with a certified teacher. I also try watching the news, though I pick up little of what is said, and attend meetings in Portuguese just for the practice. I have a grade four history reader that I am working through, which has provided good cultural learning as well as language learning.

But right now, five weeks in, I feel like I can only understand a handful of words, and can speak even fewer. I sometimes wish that I had have spent more time learning Portuguese before I came here, and other times I wish that I could just "download" the new language, Matrix-style. Language learning is certainly tough slogging. It may very well be one of the most difficult things I have ever had to do.

Of course, I am making progress. This morning, I successfully went to a photocopier store on my own and asked how much it would cost to photocopy an entire spiral-bound notebook, and then proceeded to ask the clerk to do so. All in Portuguese, without drawing my request on paper. A small victory.

It takes much time and energy to learn a language, and I have been trained to expect immediate results. Why am I not fluent in just five weeks? The truth is, I should be happy to be conversant in a couple of months.

I have sat in on several classes offered by the local Maputo City Church to teach English to Mozambicans. I have heard the people in that class labour over the pronunciation of words, seen them scratch their heads in search of their meanings, wrestle with verb conjugation, and struggle to express themselves in a brand-new language.

They see great opportunity in learning English and are extremely motivated learners. I rarely hear a word of Portuguese in those classes. What an example they set for me as I learn their language!

I have also come to realize that learning Portuguese is an exercise that pays dividends far beyond the direct benefit of being able to speak with people in their language. Mozambicans respect us for taking an interest in their culture and for investing the time needed to develop language skills. The bridge that is built through this learning experience is a healthy one: Mozambicans have the opportunity of seeing us in a position of weakness relative to themselves. They get to see the wealthy foreigner struggle. The relationships that will blossom as a result of this struggle will be well worth the effort, I trust.

A Stop Sign Means...

Yesterday we were bouncing along a poorly paved road on the edge of Maputo. Melvin, a missionary from Ireland, was driving his truck, while Laura, Raul, and I rode along. Melvin cruised right through a stop sign, slowing down only enough to make sure that crossing traffic would not be a problem.

"You have really grabbed hold of the Mozambican driving ethic, haven't you, Melvin?" I chided him. "Every time I stop at a stop sign," I continued, "Raul laughs at me and tells me that stop signs are not really for stopping, they are for slowing."

I looked over at Raul to make sure he was listening. Though he is Mozambican, Raul does not drive, so naturally Laura and I felt that our knowledge of street signs was superior to his.

"The sign says 'STOP' in English," Raul reasoned, "so that people know that it means to slow down. If they actually wanted drivers to stop, they would write it in Portuguese. *Parede.*"

We argued the logic for quite a long time, pretty much until the point that our stomachs could not handle the laughter anymore.

But underlying Raul's humorous logic was a point: why, even in a country where the official language is Portuguese, do they use the standard octagonal English stop sign? And is Raul's interpretation of a stop sign really any different than our interpretation of speed "limit" signs back home? Yes, the sign says that the limit is 100 km/h. What they really mean is 120 km/h.

My mind flashed back to a police roadside check that I had encountered in recent days. Imagine a stop sign surrounded by three police officers and a fourth sitting on a motorcycle, clearly waiting to engage in pursuit. I took my foot off the accelerator and engaged the clutch and brake, down-shifting as I approached the officers. "Why are you stopping?" my Mozambican companion asked, his voice getting a little excited. *Why would I not stop,* I wondered, but before expressing the thought, my excited companion urged me to accelerate. "Do not stop unless they tell you to!" he implored. The next two times I passed by those officers that day, I did not let up on the accelerator as I careened through the stop sign. And they did not even raise an eyebrow.

Even surrounded by police officers, a stop sign does not necessarily mean stop.

Unwanted House Guests

We have a spare bedroom in our apartment, and on some occasions we have even had the fortune of having people use it. We particularly enjoy visitors from home—not even necessarily people we know, but people passing through from familiar parts of the world.

And, this being Africa, we also have our share of unwanted house guests.

Ants are a common problem. There are hoards of them. Laura keeps a special towel in the kitchen, reserved for ant removal. My job is to remember not to dry the dishes with that one.

Potholes, Padlocks and Poverty

And we have to store all of our open food in plastic containers.

The most recent intruders have been dining away at our table for the past week, despite our best efforts to eradicate them. The termites are literally eating the wood of our kitchen table, piling crumbs of sawdust on the floor below.

We have a smaller bedside table wrapped in a garbage bag in our freezer. If the kitchen table is the termites' home, the smaller table was perhaps their summer cottage. Until it entered the deep freeze, they really liked their summer cottage. They do not help out around the house, and are really quite a nuisance. They have really been enjoying a novel Laura recently borrowed; it is such a good book that they have devoured the first 50 pages. Less than pleased, Laura opted for a new book.

There was also a time a couple of weeks ago when a gecko came to visit. The harmless lizard clung to our wall, apparently hoping that we would watch something on television, but we rarely do. When we tried to show him the door, he hid in a crevice of our sofa, so we put the whole sofa on the balcony until the gecko had moved on. (Or had he merely found a better hiding place, deeper within the chair?)

Mosquitoes are common back home, but here we have to worry about malaria, which infects nearly half a billion people a year and causes millions of deaths in this part of the world. We take precautions, but I worry about the impact on our health of those precautions, like the little chemical pads that we heat beside our bed to ward the mosquitoes off or the anti-malarial medication that can cause hallucinations.

At least they cannot be as harmful as the chemical patch I saw for sale in South Africa. The one that works by seeping repellent into your bloodstream and "turns your urine dark brown and odorous," according to the warning printed on the packaging.

And then there are times when the unwanted houseguests do

not even have the courtesy to show themselves. We just look at our arms or legs and see the little—or big—red swells that they have left behind. Little housewarming presents most recently courtesy of spiders roaming our bed while we try to sleep. Small tokens to say that they appreciate our hospitality.

Now, Unlock Your Own Mission Field

1. What kind of assistance do you think that you are called to provide: helping somebody today, or teaching them to help themselves tomorrow? Can you do one without the other? Should you?
2. How do you decide which rules are strict (stop signs) and which ones are interpreted less rigidly (speed limit signs)? Do you apply the same decision criteria to reading the Bible? How do you decide which Bible scriptures require strict enforcement and which do not?

Challenge Yourself:

Find somebody in your community who speaks a language that you do not speak. Ask that person to teach you some simple phrases. Try meeting that person in his or her space, and use your new language as much as possible.

4 Learning To Walk Humbly

October

We Are Foreigners!

Getting out of the car and going for a walk through Maputo is a great way to really catch the pulse of the city. In fact, it was while out walking this week that I made the (rather obvious) discovery that I am a foreigner.

As I walked down the street, it was hard not to think that everyone was looking at me. And truth be known, they probably were.

Skin colour is the most obvious sign of my foreignness. There is very little racial diversity in Mozambique—and, in particular, very few Caucasians. I recently wondered out loud whether or not people in Mozambique are racist. Yes, Raul assured me. Particularly in the villages, where their exposure to white people has been limited primarily to their Portuguese rulers several decades ago. In these villages, Mozambicans sometimes run at the sight of a man with light skin—perhaps assuming he is there to kidnap them or steal their land, if history is any guide.

In Maputo, people are generally more progressive. Here, my light skin is not feared but is certainly a symbol of my power and wealth. As I walk down the street, three boys stop rooting through a dumpster and look my way. One of them calls out to me, using the label "patrão." Boss. There is another word that people sometimes have for light-skinned men, again reflecting their limited exposure to our variety. On every visit to the preschool in Khongolote, I am mobbed by dozens of knee-height children chanting, "Pastore! Pastore!" That is the Portuguese word that they have discerned in their short lives to refer to men with light skin.

Sometimes I want for these people to see me as a person, not a patrão (or a pastore). The reality, though, is that the donations that Laura and I have received to pay for our living expenses this year—and drawing no salary—puts us in a league far beyond the means of most Mozambicans. Before sitting down to write, I was counting out an envelope full of cash. The envelope contained 7,800,000 meticais, which seemed like a lot in my hands but is only worth about $300. The fact that Mozambique's currency is so inflated provides a constant reality check—having nearly 8 million of anything, even if it is just meticais, makes me feel rich.

By contrast, I bought a few samosas from a lady selling them in front of her house last night. She had made them herself and was selling them for 1,000 meticais each. That is about four cents. Her day's work, if she sold all 1,000 samosas that she and her family made, would net them about $8 after expenses—which is an above-average income.

Of course, sometimes I feel like I am right back in Canada, surrounded by power structures to which I am more accustomed. A few weeks back, while I was at the Khongolote bakery buying bread for the micro-enterprise training course, I noticed that the shop employees had an old ghetto blaster playing a familiar bit of rock 'n roll—was that Bryan Adams? Yes, Bryan Adams is big in Mozambique. And yes, at least some people know that he is Canadian.

For that brief moment, I was just a regular guy standing in a bakery buying bread.

I am trying to fit in as best I can, though the barriers are huge. I need to constantly remind myself to set aside my pride in order to surmount these barriers. Nobody wears a watch, so a common way of gathering a dispersed group is to start singing. At one micro-enterprise training session, the group asked me to choose a gathering song. I quickly realized that I had to swallow my pride and pick one of two options: either sing a song that I knew (and sing alone!) or try remembering one of their songs so that they would sing along. I tried singing a Shangaan song that I had heard them sing before: "Acuna matata na jez-oo," or was it, "Nuncoona nutella and me too." Something like that. I probably sang gibberish, but they recognized the tune and (mercifully) joined in quickly.

One thing that is great about the people of Mozambique is that they are always smiling. They are always having fun. And they very graciously accept people who are obviously foreigners.

One (Tentative) Step for Microcredit

In an earlier lamentation, I expressed some frustration about the limitations of the microcredit industry in Mozambique. Specifically, I worried about the helpfulness of an industry that charges the world's poorest entrepreneurs interest rates on their loans of six percent per month and that makes credit accessible only to those with an existing business. New entrepreneurs, no matter how well thought out a business plan they may have crafted, need not apply.

Our team recently travelled to São Dâmaso to visit Cristina and Miguel, who operate a chicken farm that is small by the standards of commercial growers but sets these successful entrepreneurs in a class above many of their neighbours. Our visit has spawned the growth of an idea for tackling one of these two limitations: perhaps there is a way to leverage the expertise of successful and credit-worthy entrepreneurs like Cristina and Miguel to assist budding new entrepreneurs to start their own businesses—in this case, chicken farms.

Think of it as franchised chicken farming.

We could match people interested in starting a new business (call them franchisees) with established chicken farmers like Cristina and Miguel (the franchisors) to start a new farm. The established farmers will benefit by sharing in any profits of the new franchise; the new entrepreneurs will benefit by having access to the expertise of the successful entrepreneur, which will help them to establish and maintain successful farms and, importantly, allow them to obtain start-up capital based on the creditworthiness of the successful entrepreneur.

And more chicken in the marketplace brings more meat into protein-starved diets.

Of course, there is nothing magical about chickens. If we find established and successful coconut growers or garment makers or fishermen, the model would be the same: built around the expertise of the key people identified. Build good ideas around great people.

Once the new chicken farmers have several cycles of business experience under their figurative belts, they may choose to continue operating the chicken farming co-operative or may choose to leverage their newly established business experience to start an enterprise of their own choosing and design.

We are hoping to be able to test the model this fall, but we still have many details to work out. We also have to convince a lot of people of the merits of the model before we can implement it—not least of whom is the microcredit community.

Samuel Redux

Back in August I met Samuel, the micro-entrepreneur barber who tamed my shaggy hair. This past weekend, Laura and I got to know Samuel the student: same Samuel, different role. Samuel came knocking on our door in search of Laura, hoping that she might be able to tutor him in calculus. She willingly accepted, setting aside nearly three hours that followed to coach Samuel to a greater understanding of mathematics.

Since African society is based so heavily on relationships, we also spent considerable time just talking and getting to know him a bit better. I have often been told that when I leave Mozambique, I will measure my success by the tangible results that I achieve, but that Mozambicans will measure my success by the relationships that have been built.

At 22, Samuel is trying to finish his last year of high school this year. Final exams will start in November. Passing an exam in Mozambique too often requires payment of bribes or worse, though Samuel did not mention anything of the sort. When reflecting back upon his failed Portuguese exam of the year before, he commented only that he felt that he had done better, but that Portuguese must be more difficult than he had thought.

Students in Mozambique have only a couple hours of instruction each day to allow for the most "efficient" utilization of physical capital: typically three or four levels of classes will meet in succession in the same building, each for about three hours a day. This is essential in a country in which half the population is under 18, and many of those above 18, like Samuel, are still working to catch up on missed schooling.

Despite reduced in-class instruction, Samuel's calculus curriculum is roughly equivalent to what Laura learned at her Canadian high school. In Mozambique, students are given the basic principles and are left to sink or swim on their own. I have yet to see anyone with a textbook for any subject.

As Samuel made his way to the door, we wished him luck on his upcoming exams. *Boa sorte.* He responded with a puzzled look.

"Luck is when you are walking down the street and find money," he said. And then he continued his thought, "The only two areas in which people really need luck are opportunity and capacity. If you are lucky in these two areas, you will be successful in any other area of importance."

Opportunity and capacity. Very insightful, I thought. Too often in Canada we consider even these two areas to be fully within our control.

Samuel considers himself lucky on the first account. After his father died when Samuel was only five, his older brother travelled 1,200 kilometres north to pick him up in Nampula Province, brought him back to Maputo City, and took him in. For the next 15 years, the brother-turned-father made the sacrifices required to ensure that Samuel was properly nourished and educated. These are significant sacrifices in Mozambique, and sacrifices for which Samuel is grateful.

After high school, Samuel wants to study agriculture and then return to his birthplace of Nampula. First he needs to pass his exams and be accepted into university.

Laura surmised that Samuel was lucky on the capacity front, too. He picked up calculus fairly easily. A bright young man.

We realized that wishing someone "luck" is sort of strange, particularly for an endeavour that requires so much hard work and preparation. On his second attempt for the door, we changed our tack and conveyed our hope that Samuel would do well on his exams.

Once he was gone, we quietly hoped that he would do well in life, as well. He certainly seems to have had the good fortune of opportunity and capacity thus far.

Thanksgiving for Two

Yesterday was Thanksgiving Day in Canada, which represents the first major holiday that we are separated from our families.

Being in Mozambique and knowing no other Canadians with whom to celebrate, we feasted by ourselves.

The Canadian government formalized Thanksgiving as a holiday in 1957, naming the second Monday of October a public holiday, "for general thanksgiving to Almighty God for the blessings with which the people of Canada have been favoured." Previously, the holiday had been celebrated for numerous reasons: the end of combat, the end of cholera, the restoration of health and, most commonly, a bountiful harvest. This past week, on October 4, Mozambique held a public holiday in recognition of the 14th anniversary of the end of their civil war. Peace is still fragile, though many Mozambicans are tired of war, both in their own country and around the world. A day for giving thanks right here in Mozambique.

Despite being half a world away from Canada, this was a Thanksgiving Day for which we had many reasons to be thankful. We are in need of very little in life. Arguably nothing.

As if to emphasize the point, the electricity went out in the midst of cooking our meal. Knowing that many people in Mozambique do not have electricity and those who do see it as a bit of a luxury, we were not sure what pressure the electrical utility faces to restore the power when it goes out. Children played in the streets, oblivious to any problem. Our dinner continued to cook on our butane stove.

We feasted on the tiniest of chickens, and Laura spiced her helping with piri-piri, just to make Canadian Thanksgiving a little more Mozambican. We even stuffed the chicken with delicious dressing. For dessert we cooked a pumpkin pie, though made with butternut squash, since in Mozambique pumpkins are things only read about in used children's books donated through relief agencies. My attempt at making whipped cream, using "boxed cream" that needs no refrigeration and has a shelf life measured in months, was less than successful.

Despite being half way around the world and without family at our table, we had plenty of delicious food for our first holiday feast. I do not know why we have so much when others so close to us are hungry, but for our lot in life, we can be thankful. And for that of our neighbours, we can work towards equality.

The Limits of our Generosity

Every day we witness so many people in great need. Africa has justly earned its billing as the Earth's poor continent. We struggle with what the appropriate response might be: how can we help? How should we help?

Not a day goes by without several people asking for money. Sometimes it is people knocking on our car window at a traffic light. Often it is people trying to be productive by asking if they can guard our car or wash it.

Yesterday, a man who noticed that I was a regular at the language school called out to me in English, "Boss, tomorrow you wash my car?" (I am pretty sure he meant the other way around, but maybe I should bring my rag and bucket today just to be sure.) I replied, "Of course."

Another man who recently washed our car did so with the same rag and bucket that he had been using for days. When he was done, the car looked like he had smeared around the existing dirt and added a little of his own for good measure.

We get our car washed often.

There are so many people looking for help. Many people are not lazy; there are not many jobs to be found, and the country is struggling to catch up on educating a population frozen in time by civil war.

At home, we often found ourselves screening people before giving them money. If you are asking for my money, you had better look like you are going to spend it on food, not alcohol.

As Westerners, we often prefer to give anonymously through large charitable organizations that will make sure that our contributions are being put to good use. Doing so also gets us an accounting of our year's generosity and a tax receipt so that we can get some of it back.

The Bible challenges us to give without judgment. It challenges us to give to anyone who asks, without evaluating whether or not their need surpasses an arbitrary threshold that we have established in our minds. It challenges us to give, even if the person asking might not use our gift in a way that we would consider to be appropriate: *Give to the one who asks you, and do not turn away from the one who wants to borrow from you* (Matthew 5:42). That sounds a little bit counter-cultural, does not it? Our culture teaches us that, being the possessors of our wealth, we have the right to make the final determination about who needs our benevolence and who does not.

African culture flips this on its head. The person requesting something plays a major role in determining whether his or her need is greater than that of the potential donor. If someone is asking me for money in Africa, it is not only because they have a great need for it, but also because they have concluded that my money would do greater good to them than it would to me.

And almost without exception, they are right. Here, the poverty is so gripping. When we walk our trash out to the dumpster, there are always a couple of men who quietly take our bags from us. They have sorted through the dumpster and have taken anything of value: any rotten fruit or mouldy bread that may have been discarded. They will look through our bags, too, before they place them in the dumpster.

Imagine having to live off of the refuse of the world's poorest.

Nobody deserves to live that kind of life. We have decided to bring along some extra fruit or bread whenever we take out our garbage. These men have yet to thank us for it, but we do not do it for our own reward.

If I have one less dollar, or one less loaf of bread, or one less banana, it has very little impact on my life. If the average Mozambican had one more of any of these, it would mean that she could feed her children today. Economists call this marginal benefit.

We are still struggling with how we can help, but for now we have decided that African culture and Christianity are in agreement on this point: if someone asks us for something, we will give it.

And Christianity would suggest that we should do so back home in Canada, too.

A Day to Honour Samora Machel

It is amazing how many times over the past couple of months we have shook our heads saying, "This just does not happen at home...."

Today is just another one of those days.

Yesterday, I was thinking about how busy my day today was going to be. I already had a couple of meetings scheduled, plus Portuguese lessons, when the director of Laura's school asked me to fill in for a sick teacher.

All of that changed by mid-afternoon, when rumours started circulating that the government had declared the following day—today—to be a national holiday. How can a government declare a holiday less than 12 hours before it starts? How will everyone be informed? Do not businesses and schools need to prepare to be closed?

In Mozambique, people have a way of knowing. Rumours about holidays spread through the city like a grassfire on the dry savannah. As one young man, Timóteo, explained to me, "We Mozambicans like our holidays." I cannot argue with that.

Timóteo proceeded to make a second noteworthy observation: patting his stomach, he said, "Unfortunately, this thing never goes on holiday." In Mozambique, where much of the workforce is informal, people are paid by the hour or by the job. When they are forced to take the day off, they are not paid. But they still must eat. And they still must pay their bills.

Sometimes holidays are only a blessing for the wealthy and the salaried.

Twenty years ago, October 19, 1986, Samora Machel, the first president of the independent Republic of Mozambique, died when his plane crashed in the hills of South Africa. There is no official explanation for the cause of the crash, but just ask any Mozambican what happened and you will hear the same story: South Africa's apartheid government, under President P. W. Botha, planted a false beacon in the hills, steering the plane off course and causing it to crash into the hillside.

Samora Machel is still seen as somewhat of a national hero, albeit a controversial one. For today's celebration, the government hung banners in the streets reminiscent of Machel's tenure as president of a socialist state struggling against capitalism. This banner stretched across Avenida Vladimir Lenine, near our apartment:

"SAMORA COMMITS US TO CONTINUE THE
STRUGGLE UNTIL THE FINAL VICTORY."

When I asked my friend Mario about Samora Machel, he spoke with a bit of admiration and even romanticism in his voice—similar to the way in which he speaks of his deceased father.

I cannot argue with the purpose of the holiday. I just would have thought that the government would have seen this twentieth anniversary coming and could have planned ahead a bit further. But that is not the African way.

Church-Raising in São Dâmaso

This weekend, Laura and I decided to venture out of the city. It is always a bit of an ordeal since beyond the edge of Maputo all but the main roads are paved with loosely packed sand, so we have to borrow a vehicle with four-wheel drive to make the journey. Our destination was a small church in a community called São Dâmaso, about 45 minutes outside of Maputo, whose two leaders I met during our micro-enterprise training in Khongolote a couple of months ago. They invited us to visit, and we are finally taking them up on their offer.

For the past two years, the church in São Dâmaso has operated out of a small building on rented land. Earlier this year, they purchased their own land nearby and—because caniço (reeds) is a wonderfully portable construction material—took the church apart, carried it down the street, and reassembled it on their newly acquired property. A group of five people from Oregon who were here visiting this week helped with the project. The labourers took the opportunity to install more durable posts and roof struts so that, over time, they can replace the church's reed walls with concrete blocks to make their building more permanent and weather-resistant.

Some of the caniço wall panels needed to be replaced, but in a society that wastes little, the old walls still had value. Nelson, the church's leader, wanted to put them to use to enclose his outdoor washroom. We hoisted them onto the roof of our borrowed Land Cruiser and bounced our way to Khongolote, where Nelson lives with his wife and children in a small home built by an international aid agency after Mozambique's floods in 2000.

Relationship and community are immensely important attributes in Africa, and the home is an important focal point of these relationships. In fact, there is a saying here that if you do not know my house, you do not know me. At the conclusion of the church meeting in São Dâmaso, every single member in attendance, bar none—perhaps 20 or 30 people in all—walked to the home of a woman who was too ill to attend. There they crowded into her living room, spent 15 minutes in song and prayer to show their support and hope for healing, and then parted ways. Their act of kindness required an investment of only 15 minutes, but I am sure it brightened that lady's entire day.

Congratulations, Dr. Yunus, But...

Earlier this month, the Norwegian Nobel Committee—that illustrious black box that decides who is worthy of the Nobel prizes each year—decided that the 2006 Nobel Peace Prize would be awarded to Muhammad Yunus, widely regarded as the founder of microcredit, and his Grameen Bank.

As part of the official announcement, the committee noted that, "Every single individual on earth has both the potential and the right to live a decent life." Both the potential and the right. Nobody deserves to live a life of poverty, and Dr. Yunus has dedicated his life to ensuring that fewer do.

This award is a wonderful way to recognize his efforts in this regard.

But he should not be content to accept this award as the end of a great accomplishment; it is merely the beginning. We should applaud Dr. Yunus' achievements with the encouraging intent of a parent watching her child take a first step. What the parent really wants is for the child to have the courage to take a second, and then a third.

The Norwegian Nobel Committee recognizes this. That is why, according to popular speculation, such hopefuls as former Finnish President Martti Ahtisaari (who brokered peace between

Indonesia's government and Aceh separatists in August 2005) were passed over for this year's award. Mr. Ahtisaari's work was done; the sharp minds on the Nobel Committee saw no need to encourage further progress.

Dr. Yunus, your work is not done. You know that better than I do. Let us ensure that the rest of the world understands this award to be a carrot tempting us all to further progress, not a retrospective "lifetime achievement award" for the nascent microcredit industry.

In Bangladesh and elsewhere, the microcredit industry has detractors. People think that the interest rates are still too high. Nowhere is that more true than in Mozambique, where poor entrepreneurs are asked to pay back their loans plus six percent each month.

Sure, the bath water may be dirty, but that is no reason to toss the baby.

December 10, the anniversary of the death of Alfred Nobel, is the traditional day for distribution of the Nobel awards. Dr. Yunus, I implore you to use your acceptance speech on this day as an opportunity to showcase the steps that have yet to be taken.

Congratulations, Dr. Yunus, but there is more work to be done.

Debunking the Fallacy of "Limited Good"

Some people might be wondering why I spend so much time learning culture and language while in Mozambique. After all, if my wife and I are only spending a year here, would success not be easier to come by if I just focused on the task at hand? The reality is that success will not be possible unless I learn the culture of Mozambique as fully and completely as possible. A cultural lesson that I learned this week highlights this fact.

The people of Mozambique ascribe to a concept called *limited good*: that everything, whether tangible (such as wealth) or intangible (such as happiness), is in limited supply, and that one person having an abundance of anything means that someone else will be lacking in it. All facets of life are seen as zero-sum; life is set up as a jealous rivalry. If I have more health or wealth or happiness than my neighbour, he will perceive that I have stolen his share of it.

At first thought, this seems like a strange idea. Free-market capitalist societies have as a central tenet that wealth is in unlimited supply; that it can be and is created (albeit not distributed evenly) every day. Upon further reflection, one must admit that the idea of limited good lurks just beneath the surface even in our own culture. It rears its head in the form of jealousy when a colleague gets a coveted promotion, or when a neighbour buys a shiny new car, or when a friend is publicly recognized for a good deed.

The theory of limited good has profound implications for our chicken farming idea, and for economic development projects in general. If our project is to be successful, we need to create the conditions necessary to avoid both jealousy on the part of those who do not participate and a deliberate undermining of success on the part of those selected in an effort to avoid standing out from the pack. It makes no difference whether or not the theory is true; because people believe it, their actions will be shaped by it.

The collective nature of African culture prevents individuals from wanting to distance themselves from their neighbours. Those who do find success may fear recrimination from jealous family and witchcraft-practicing neighbours. Raul, one of the church leaders that I work with, recently bought a plot of land beyond the suburbs of Maputo, even though the church he leads is in the heart of the city. He wanted to be as far away as practical, not so that he could afford a sprawling property and a suburban-lifestyle home, but because he wanted to hide his possession behind the obscurity that great distance provides. He did not want to stand out from the norm of his congregation and peers, many of whom cannot afford to purchase a home of their own.

We should never doubt that the intangibles—things like happiness, even our own salvation—are in limitless supply. God permits—indeed, God wants—all of us to live good and righteous lives. If the concept of limited good is applied to these intangibles, it serves only to drive a wedge between ourselves and God in an effort to preserve harmony among people. If instead we could recognize that "good" is not a commodity in limited supply, we would all be better neighbours and global citizens.

If the people of Mozambique could realize that good begets good, they may be more motivated to lift themselves out of the proverbial muck.

Now, Unlock Your Own Mission Field

1. What judgments do you make of people who ask you for handouts? What conditions or evaluation criteria do you use to accept or reject their requests?
2. Do you believe that there is a limited or an unlimited amount of "good" in the world? How do you react to the success of those around you? How do those around you react to your own success?

Challenge Yourself:

Provide fifteen minutes of kindness to somebody to whom you would not ordinarily have reached out. Buy them a coffee and ask how they are doing. Rake their leaves or shovel the snow from their driveway. Meet them at the place of their need.

5 Anchoring Our Vision

100 Days

Today is our 100th day in Mozambique. In some ways, it is hard to imagine that 100 days have passed already. In other ways, it seems that we have been here a lifetime.

After a new president or prime minister has taken office, he or she is often asked to sit down and reflect upon the first 100 days of their mandate. Time to take stock. Following that time-honoured tradition, I woke up early this morning and peeked outside. No media trucks. I checked my phone for messages. No interviews scheduled. Just as well, I suppose. But that does not mean that I cannot pause here and take stock of these first 100 days.

My temptation is to zoom out and look at the macro view first. In what tangible, lasting way have I changed the continent in these first 100 days? Or at least improved the future of this country?

Sounds unrealistic, doesn't it? A little ridiculous. Yet that is the standard we hold our political leaders to and one that has been engrained in my being. Our Western culture teaches us to "swing for the fence" and to "catch the big fish." We glorify rapid and large-scale success.

I beat myself up for not having solved an intractable, complicated problem that millions of people and billions of dollars have been chipping away at for generations.

A healthier perspective is to zoom in and focus on the micro view. In what ways has being here had an impact on someone's life?

How have I moved the yardsticks forward for one person in Mozambique?

How have I moved the yardsticks forward for one person back home?

And how have I moved them forward in my own life?

Some sceptics may think that is a cop-out, that I am lowering expectations to ensure that I am able to meet them. I do not see it that way at all. And the lady with the fruit stand down the street does not see it that way, either. The one who smiles and waves every day and who is pleased to sell me tomatoes and green peppers, but only after she asks me about my day and if my parents are healthy.

I came to Mozambique to bring poverty relief through economics. I came hoping to leave lives in a bit better state. I came so that people might see that I love them because God first loved me.

And no doubt, I will leave having accomplished some of that.

But there is nothing more enriching in African culture than the value of personal relationships. There is nothing more enriching than just being with somebody. (And that is a hard and tiring lesson for this introvert to learn!)

I would be foolish to try to fight poverty but forsake the poor.

What has changed in these first 100 days? Perhaps nothing as great as my perspective on people in poverty: they are people foremost and do not define themselves by their poverty.

A Spirited Opposition

Late last week, I had the opportunity of presenting our chicken-farming strategy to a gathering of Mozambican church leaders: people like Raul, Nelson, and Ricardo. We try to work through this group, encouraging them to take ownership of projects rather than doing them ourselves, empowering Mozambicans to help Mozambicans. We try to "lead from the side," building their leadership capacity, hoping to work ourselves out of a job. If these leaders are not willing to endorse our projects, we reason, then neither will they take sufficient responsibility over them to ensure their success.

Strangely enough, the prospect of facing these $1-a-day men caused my heart to beat a little harder than normal. It was reminiscent of the countless times that I have sat across a table from a committee of high-powered politicians back home presenting recommendations for the direction of our province. In both cases, I must admit to a little anxiety.

And in both cases, the scrutiny was trying. The questions they asked were difficult, and they did not always like my answers. I wished that I had have done a little more homework. There is always a little more to do.

On some level, I was glad for their combativeness. Had I expected to have come riding in on a horse from stage right to save the poor Africans from their plight? They are still living, breathing, critically thinking human beings.

For hours they asked questions. I tried to understand in Portuguese and asked for translation when I needed to catch a nuance. I usually responded in English because the translator had a better chance of accurately conveying my thoughts.

Maybe the translation was the problem. Not the words, but the barrier of suspicion that naturally divides people speaking through the help of an intermediary. I wished that I could have spoken fluent Portuguese. Better yet, Shangaan. At least the translator was an insider, known to the group and myself.

Through the fog of my frustration, their questions seemed to boil down to plain selfishness. We were presenting a proposal for franchised chicken farms to benefit the communities in which their churches are located. Not restricted to church members, and certainly not restricted to church leaders.

They wanted to redesign the program to deliver employment opportunities for themselves first and foremost. And they did not want to take a loan from an arms-length microcredit organization, as our proposal suggested. Their reasons were numerous, many valid. The subtext was that they wanted me to provide the money, no interest required, and no risk required. I would not force repayment because I belong to a Christian organization, they silently reasoned.

All of their criticisms were carefully addressed in a business plan that we had prepared for their input. Sure, microcredit interest rates are high, for example, but the plan takes that into account and still shows a reasonable profit for owner-workers.

Their counter-proposal, not so much spoken as implied, was that they would take our money, try their hands at raising chickens, and if they ever found themselves better off than us, they could give us our money back. They pressed for a handout.

Knowing that many of them would not have had eaten yet that day, I brought a bag full of oranges and passed them around. The group then passed around a machete that they used to peel the oranges and threw their peels into a plastic bucket in the centre of the ring of blue wooden benches that we were perched atop. (Okay, so there were some differences between facing these guys and facing the committee of politicians back home!)

I brought one orange too few, so did not take one myself. Nelson, generous in spirit and seeing me as an equal, peeled his orange, broke it in two, and offered me half. These are people with big hearts, but imbued with a strong survival instinct. After all, they are hungry and poor. In their situation, I cannot say that I would not press for a handout with an equal amount of zeal.

In fact, they probably interpret my unwillingness to capitulate and provide a gift as my own lack of a generous spirit.

To many, providing a handout may seem like a logical response to economic injustice in Africa, especially when poverty is viewed as a lack of resources. Is not the best way to fight poverty to do so with money?

But handouts do not empower people to help themselves in the long-run. Worse, they are not even neutral, but sap the motivation to take necessary and healthy risks required to get ahead. Having received handouts in the past, they expect handouts to continue in the present. Anything less than a direct gift is rejected.

Nobel laureate Muhammad Yunus, in his autobiography, *Banker to the Poor*, makes the following statement about the applicability of microcredit in contexts with a strong social safety net:

> [M]*y great nemesis is the tenacity of the social welfare system. Over and over,* [microcredit projects] *have run into the same problem: recipients of a monthly handout from the government...calculate the amount of welfare money and insurance coverage they would lose by becoming self-employed and conclude the risk is not worth the effort.*[3]

In Mozambique, there is no government social safety net, but handouts from foreign governments and non-governmental organizations, including our own, have created the same mix of dependency, complacency, and expectancy. In the long run, people will benefit from being empowered to help themselves. But the prospect of not receiving another handout is a bitter pill that they are being asked to swallow.

---

[3] Yunus, *Banker to the Poor,* pp 189-190.

In a gesture to ensure that relationships were preserved in the face of the difficult meeting, one of the church leaders came up to me afterwards and apologized for the feisty spirit of the group. "But it was your own fault," he said. "Your oranges gave us energy."

And then, to make sure I knew he was joking he added, "Next time, you should bring ice cream."

Wedding Bells in Khongolote

Wedding bells chimed in Mozambique for Paulo and Olga this weekend, figuratively speaking, anyway, and Laura and I travelled to Khongolote to witness the nuptials.

The wedding ceremony was scheduled to begin at 11:30am. On our way to the ceremony, our colleague Melvin, who was driving us, got a telephone call from Raul, hoping we could give him a ride. That would save him the trouble of catching a chapa (the local minivan transit service). Even though it was already 11:10am and Khongolote was another 30 minutes away, we circled back to pick him up.

When we finally arrived at noon, we were surprised to find the wedding had already started. Meetings never run on time, and even less so weddings. In fact, weddings are notoriously late in part because the groom must first make a trip to the provincial capital of Matola to take care of the legal documentation. The length of the wait at the government office in Matola is unpredictable.

Weddings also tend to run long. We witnessed some potential causes for that: first there were the congregation members who felt that certain songs needed to be sung, even if they were not agreed to in advance and printed in the program. They would just start belting them out from their pews, and everyone would happily join along. Almost everyone. Even in Africa, some people were seen rolling their eyes.

Next were the people who walked up to the front of the church to provide miniature soliloquies. Since they were in Shangaan, we did not know what wisdom the speakers were imparting on the newlyweds, but hoots and guffaws emanated from the benches all around us. The presiding church leader stood up and sat down several times, casting his eyes about, unsure of what would happen next.

The wedding included an interesting mix of African and Western culture. The bride wore a wedding dress that is shared around the community for such occasions. Same for the suits that the men wore. And there was an exchange of wedding bands, which, since I have yet to see anyone wearing rings, may have been borrowed as well.

We stayed after the ceremony for the reception, which was a late lunch of rice, beans, and chicken or fish. A guest on my right found a chicken foot in his rice. The young boy on my left protested to his parents as a fish's head glared up at him from his bowl. The guests of honour at the head table received special luxuries, like bottles of Coke and Fanta. Nobody left hungry.

All of the guests were packed tightly into rows of the ubiquitous blue benches. Weddings are fancy, but the community has limits. The guests ate out of plastic bowls, which we balanced on our laps, since we did not have tables. Most of us were given one piece of cutlery to use. Some a fork, others a spoon. Even with this rationing, there were not enough utensils to go around, so some people used their fingers.

After the meal, groups of people sang and danced their way to the head table to present gifts to the newlyweds. The gifts were simple: a group of a dozen women purchased a box of patio glasses, and each woman presented one glass to the couple. Another group presented a set of pots and pans, each woman waving a pot or a pan or a lid or a spoon as she danced.

The newly wed couple have been socialized not to smile at such a serious affair as a wedding, though their guests had a boisterous time.

At the end of the celebration, the couple was chauffeured away in a small white Toyota, spinning its tires on the rain-soaked mud roads. We followed behind in a four-by-four truck, going very slowly. When Melvin, who was driving our truck, suggested passing the bride and groom, the Mozambicans in our car were shocked. Pass a bride and groom on their wedding day? Bad luck, I guess.

We turned down a side street and sped away.

A Second Step Forward

Despite the challenges encountered when I presented our chicken-farming strategy to church leaders, this week I returned with my colleague Glenn to present the idea to Cristina and Miguel, the family of chicken farmers who could potentially serve as the "franchisor" in our model, and received a more positive reception.

Since we had been at their home a couple of weeks ago, they had expanded their chicken houses and were now raising 2,150 chickens—roughly a 100 percent increase. We were encouraged by their success. Miguel explained to us that they expanded because they saw greater demand for their product. He also explained that entrepreneurs never stop expanding. He is not satisfied with 2,150 chickens, but wants to grow the business even larger.

That sentiment is the fuel that drives economic development around the world. These seem like great mentors and teachers, if only they would be willing to share their knowledge with would-be entrepreneurs. It is also the sentiment that we are hoping to build upon for the success of our franchise farming model. Cristina and Miguel have a vision of us helping them to expand their business by building more chicken houses and buying more chickens; by contrast, our vision is to help them expand by teaching them to sell the expertise that they have developed over the past decade of raising chickens to help inexperienced franchisees to have the same success.

Cristina and Miguel received the proposal in a very encouraging manner: sceptical optimism. They welcomed the proposal, and thought that it was a good idea. They also spoke at length about a list of fears that they have.

Of their fears, trust was featured most prominently. "How can we trust the franchisees," they asked. "What if they steal our chickens?" "What if they do not work hard?" These are valid concerns. We cannot assure them that the franchisees are worthy of their trust, but we can provide Cristina and Miguel the opportunity to meet any potential franchisees before committing to move forward with the project. After all, they are the ones who need to trust their franchisees; not us.

They also spoke about assuming additional risk by bringing outsiders into their already-successful operation.

And they shared with us the story of a woman who had found business success, only to be poisoned to death by envious clients.

I was glad that they shared these fears with us. Their sharing signalled that they trust us enough to be honest with us. It also signalled that they are engaging the proposal seriously enough to properly weigh its risks and benefits.

I am not an expert at reading this foreign culture. It had occurred to me that their response might be the polite, indirect way of turning down our proposal, but I do not think so. And neither did our interpreter.

A second step forward.

Next, we have to bring the idea back to the church leaders. If they again demonstrate reticence, we may have to build some momentum by proving the concept using a more willing group of people, in a different village.

Potholes, Padlocks and Poverty

As we wrapped up the meeting and were about to begin our drive back into the city, Miguel walked around back of his house and soon re-emerged with a live chicken under his arm. A gift to express his appreciation for us and our work. We politely declined their generous offer, sheepishly admitting that we did not know how to prepare a live chicken. His wife laughed at us, and insisted that we return to their house some day to feast on that chicken together. She would even teach us how to kill and prepare it. I will never turn down an invitation to a barbecue, but I hope next time to bring with me several potential franchisees to share the feast and begin building the bonds of trust.

Can Helping Hurt?

We have decided to help people however and wherever asked. So what is the proper response when someone makes a request that could easily be fulfilled, but might just end up hurting more than helping?

Yesterday morning a friend approached me and asked for a loan. To me, it was a relatively small sum: I could have honoured his request for $250. And through the looking-glass of North America, the need seemed great: he wanted the money to buy some sheets of tin to cover his open-to-the-sky house and some cement blocks to close in a gaping hole in his front wall. How can I deny someone $250 so that he can literally put a roof over his head?

To him, by contrast, this request was huge. It represented several months' worth of salary.

Although I have been to his house several times, I do not really understand his living conditions. I do not really understand what it is like to have to cook out in the rain, or to have to try to sleep amongst the drips of condensation falling from the tin ceiling on an otherwise dry night. But I also know that he has lived without much of his house covered since June (which is not that unusual in

Mozambique), so I know that the situation was not urgent. Important, yes. Urgent, no.

When presented with the request, I told this young Mozambican man that I would consider his request and that we could talk about it the next day. When we met again this morning, I did not have an answer, but instead had prepared a lesson on Biblically sound financial principles.

My task when I came to Mozambique was to work on micro-enterprise development initiatives. Being here, I have realized that mentoring people on personal finances is a critically important foundational step: an entrepreneur cannot build a successful business if he does not know how to manage his own finances. The requester is a young Christian, so respected the wisdom of the Bible. Had he not been, its teachings are still rational, rooted in common sense.

I spoke to him about things that seem obvious to a guy with a Master's degree in business, a house with a mortgage, and a family to feed. I asked him questions like:

Have you made a plan? Do you really need to do all of the work now? Or can some of it wait until you have saved some money?

How will you continue to feed yourself and your family—an important obligation—if you spend several months of salary on these house improvements?

How will you cope with other unexpected expenses that may arise over the coming months?

How will taking this loan restrict your future decisions? Will it require you to continue along a path you do not like in order to pay the loan back? Might it prevent you from pursuing an opportunity that arises because of the outstanding obligation?

These questions struck him as great bits of wisdom, though he confessed to me later that he thought I was just trying to find an excuse to cling to my money. He understood the need to think carefully about his request and asked for time to do so.

Naturally, I could have offered to give him the money, which would seem like the compassionate thing to do. That would have been completely within my ability, and it is a response that I wrestled with at great length.

I could have allowed him to put a roof over his house and avoid being enslaved by debt.

My hope is that mentoring him in the way to plan and think through his financial decisions will be an investment worth far more to him than had I opened my wallet and handed him $250. My prayer is that he becomes a master of his own destiny, not dependent upon the generosity of a rich, white foreigner next time a big financial need arises.

I do not yet know how I will help. This friend will soon return to me, having carefully reconsidered his request. I expect that he will come back to me with a proposal—perhaps the same request, perhaps not. And if, when he returns, he again requests the loan, should I comply?

The Longer It Takes, the More We Will Earn

Maputo is a sprawling city whose many low-rise concrete buildings are due for more than just a fresh coat of paint. Much of the city was built by the Portuguese, and when they fled (which coincided with Mozambique's independence in 1975), they left behind a void of professionals and skilled trades workers. Buildings that were under construction 30 years ago remain unfinished, though where possible completed floors are occupied.

This is not to say that people in Mozambique lack the capacity to build and maintain major infrastructure works, rather, that it is incumbent upon the leadership of a nation to train up its people with the requisite skills to do so. The country's colonizers withheld such education in decades passed, and Mozambique still suffers for it.

The organization that we are attached to while in Mozambique is developing a post-secondary institution that will offer seminary training to aspiring pastors. By North American standards, the project is relatively small: once completed, it will be a 15,000 square foot, four-storey concrete block and glass structure. Not unusual anywhere in the world, the project is behind schedule by several months. In fact, by the original schedule it should have been completed before I arrived in Mozambique. At the request of the project manager, I have offered a hand in my spare moments to help keep the project moving along, and working on site has provided me a telling glimpse into how business is conducted in Africa.

The most immediate difference between construction sites in Maputo and those back home is that, here, safety regulations appear almost non-existent. I have seen a hard hat on the construction site once, upside down, full of water, being used by a worker to clean his tools. Steel-toed boots are evidently not required; construction workers show up to work variably in worn sneakers (sometimes with their toes poking through) or cheap plastic flip-flops. And there is no heavy equipment on site: a few months back, a cement pump truck was used, but just as common is the sight of workers milling about with buckets of cement or paint or tile adhesive.

These workers have a very real and immediate need to feed their families. Payment upon completion of a job is not always practical because the workers' families are quite literally hungry. Payment in small amounts—even $20 at a time—keeps bellies full, spirits high, and maintains the project's momentum. The project manager is constantly making these microscopic payments in order to grease the wheels of progress. And because business is transacted largely in cash, these payments require a strong record-keeping discipline. Imagine trying to build a house or an office tower without conducting an electronic funds transfer or writing a single cheque.

Several contracts with sub-contractors are for labour only, making it our responsibility to ensure that materials are present—a risk they will not accept because of the difficulty in securing the proper materials and because they do not have sufficient working capital to carry an inventory. If the foreman receives a small payment, he is just as likely to use it to buy food and drink as he is to buy materials needed to finish the job. Most recently, the labourers who have been hired to lay tile on the hallway floors and bathroom walls ran out of materials earlier this week. I travelled with an assistant to nearly a dozen shops over two days before finding tiles—similar in colour, and not quite the right size. But close enough to keep pressing forward.

Despite these challenges, the construction continues on, albeit at a Mozambican pace. After visiting the 12th building supply shop, I returned with Geraldo, our Mozambican project assistant, with my small car loaded with enough tile and grout to keep the workers busy for a few more days. When we arrived, the tile setters were sitting around playing a game of checkers—one side using bottle caps, another side using small stones. Geraldo called them over to collect the new materials, yelling some of the only words he knows in English: "Come on! Time is money!" He looked at me and laughed, wondering if I had ever heard that expression. The tile setters would not have understood the words, and even if they had have been in Portuguese, they would not have understood their significance.

"I heard someone yell that in South Africa once," Geraldo explained to me, with a grin on his face. "Those guys work hard."

The Response

A weekend has passed, and my friend who had requested a loan to put a roof over his head returned and told me that he had done much thinking, and would still like the full loan, if I am able to offer it to him.

Of course, the rules of the game shifted over the weekend.

As if to taunt the "wisdom" of my earlier words, my prospective borrower's house was robbed on the very day I wrote them. His repairs were important, yes; urgent, no, I wrote. And then the very vulnerability that he sought to repair was breached.

As I was typing, thieves were walking through the hole in his wall and into his house. The target of the thievery was not televisions or jewellery. He does not have these things. He does not even have electricity or running water. No, the target had basic, but real, value. My friend was robbed of his single-burner paraffin stove, a pan full of food, and some other food on shelves. The thief was hungry.

How much this theft impacted my friend's decision to take the loan, I will never know.

After much deliberation, I decided to meet him part way. I loaned him a third of the money that he needed, and the two of us agreed to a schedule of weekly repayments. I also gave him another third outright as an early Christmas bonus for work that he has been doing for me over the past months. Needing the final third will keep him motivated to continue to chase down leads for more regular work.

I also offered to help him with the repairs.

He was quite happy with this outcome. The schedule of repayment contemplates him being able to pay off the debt in two months. It is a little bit aggressive, but he welcomed the challenge. He pointed to one week in the middle of the schedule, and announced his goal to double his payment for that week in order to pay off the debt faster. In doing so, he figured that $16 a month was more than what he needed to buy rice, cooking oil and sugar. The Mozambican staples. He would find a way to survive.

And he had understood that debt is serious after all.

The Vision Thing

During the recent meeting with church leaders in which I faced opposition to our business ideas, one person raised a simple but important question: "What is the vision for this project?" he asked. His vision and mine did not match, which made me realize that I need to spend more time articulating and selling a clear vision. Let me back-track a bit.

The objective for my work in Mozambique is to identify and remove any barriers that exist to economic development for members of our churches and their communities. This objective will be accomplished in three ways:

• Micro-enterprise training and mentoring opportunities, including financial stewardship and accountability at personal, church, and business levels;

• Facilitating access to business opportunities and resources, including business franchising opportunities; and,

• Promotion of village-based savings and credit services.

I have experimented with micro-enterprise training already. The response has been that training needs to be accompanied by financial resources to implement new business ideas. I then moved to franchise chicken farming but, as the church leaders pointed out, the same problems exist: many Mozambicans are not willing to accept the options for financing that they are able to access. The first two components of our strategy will be put on the back burner until a foundation of savings and credit services acceptable to Mozambicans has been established. This is the third component.

Since coming to Mozambique, I have realized that we cannot remove barriers to economic development simply by starting yet another microcredit bank. There are an abundance of microfinance institutions working here already. Thirty-two, by last count. Several of them are sophisticated, international organizations whose core business is the financial services that they provide.

Credit is available, albeit at a high price, to those who want it, particularly in urban areas.

Many proponents of microcredit like to simplify the world into two groups: those who are thriving with microcredit loans and those who have not yet received microcredit loans.

Africa is more complex than this.

The challenges are clear: well-established microcredit banks have come to the conclusion that microcredit lending is extremely expensive and have reflected that conclusion in their interest rates.

As well, Mozambique's credit culture is sufficiently weak that many people readily interpret loans—particularly loans from deep pocketed Westerners—to be grants. Gifts to be repaid only in the event that the borrower becomes wealthier than the lender. Gifts, in all likelihood, that will never have to be repaid.

The third component, then, cannot simply be accomplished by the creation of another microcredit bank. This will not resolve the underlying problems that we have faced. A better model for the people we want to target is to start building a savings infrastructure so that people can accumulate wealth. They can do this amongst themselves, as a group. When people need to borrow, they can borrow from the group's pool, and pay a modest amount of interest that is in turn given to deposit holders. People will not object as strongly to paying interest to themselves and their neighbours as to the BMW-driving microcredit bank operator in the city.

It is really a model of grassroots banking. It will be slow to implement, since no loans will be paid out until savings have been received, but it will be more sustainable. Our role will be to train Mozambicans with the process and structure and let them implement it. They will not need us to maintain a complex or expensive banking infrastructure. And we will not need to provide funding ourselves and struggle down the road with damage to our churches and relationships by needing to deal with repayment problems.

This vision, I would argue, is quite bold and exciting. The vision means that Mozambicans can make donor-driven micro-credit lending obsolete by filling their own savings and credit needs until those needs are large and sophisticated enough to qualify for commercial banking. The model that I am proposing is neither new nor perfect. In some ways, it mirrors important features of the Grameen bank that have been removed by its successors, chief amongst which is ownership by the borrowers.

Our vision is to fight poverty by giving power back to the people.

Now, Unlock Your Own Mission Field

1. Read Micah 6:8, and then think of a particular instance in which you have been faced with a difficult request or decision. What would your response have been if you acted justly? What if you acted mercifully? In what ways are these responses different?
2. Think about a recent time when people have rejected your ideas or opinions. How did you respond? What conditions or experiences might have led them to have this perspective?

Challenge Yourself:

Find a group or organization in your community that needs your hands, not your wallet. Pick up a hammer for Habitat for Humanity. Mobilize your community for a 30-Hour Famine. Dish out a meal at a local soup kitchen. Tutor a child struggling to keep up in school.

6 A Stripped-Down Holiday Season

Today is World AIDS Day

Last week, as I stood talking with one of the workers at the seminary construction site, he looked down at a cut on his hand, and wiped the blood onto his pants. Mozambique is generally among the top ten countries ranked by HIV/AIDS prevalence. The remaining nine are Mozambique's sub-Saharan neighbours.

The first thought that ran through my mind was, "I need rubber gloves." The stigma of the disease says that its sufferers are untouchable. In Mozambique, where the HIV/AIDS prevalence rate is 50 times that of Canada, people do not think about basic things like rubber gloves.

AIDS is a disease exacerbated by poverty. Poor mothers cannot afford the medication that would reduce the risk of transferring the disease to her children during birth. Even when they receive these medications free of charge, they often cannot afford the balanced and regular diet required to optimize the drugs' effectiveness.

And it is a disease that perpetuates poverty. Imagine a work-force in which one out of every seven people has this one disease. That is the situation in Mozambique. Now imagine the number of additional people who miss work regularly in order to look after loved ones who are sick. And imagine the number of orphaned

91

children who can no longer afford to attend school, starting their lives at a disadvantage.

We have seen homes where AIDS has cruelly thrust head of the household responsibility upon a seven-year-old child. A seven-year-old child struggling to be an adult.

Despite having lived in Mozambique for over four months, I have only experienced the ravages of this pandemic indirectly: through conversations about its impact, through advertisements, through stories. This might partly be my fault, not having picked up on cultural cues. People sometimes refer to it ominously as "the sickness." And rightfully so: it is the cause underlying one death out of every four here in Mozambique.

It has also driven the life expectancy rate down by three years since 1999. Here in Mozambique, people can now only expect to live to be 38 years old. And that rate continues to fall.

Thankfully, I have not yet known anyone here to have died as a result of AIDS. That fact alone, perhaps more than any other, makes me a stranger in this land.

Going Postal

I cannot think of a government bureaucracy as oft-maligned the world over as the postal service. Particularly in the heady days of electronic communication, people often wondered aloud not only when but if their "snail mail" parcels would ever arrive.

Oh, how we love to make sport of berating the postal service!

In Mozambique, there exists no such luxury as door-to-door mail delivery. In our apartment, we have an often rain-soaked pile downstairs at the common entrance, and that serves as our "mail box." Some companies that want to deliver to us personally, such as our internet service provider, hire their own courier staff to deliver bills. Others, such as the telephone utility, just throw the lot of bills on top of the soggy heap on the ground floor.

And they do not bother using envelopes. Imagine the laments of privacy advocates if they were to find a stack of papers itemizing everyone's personal telephone calls sitting in that pile for all to see!

I needed to mail some letters recently, so I asked the natural question: where can I buy stamps around here? A litany of supplemental questions flooded into my head: Where can I drop my mail? Where is the post office? Will this even work?

The post office, I was informed, is at the airport. That is good. My letter will be as close as possible to the airplane that will take it to Canada.

It also made sense: locals do not seem to use the postal service. There is no door-to-door delivery, and they would not want to spend their little bit of money mailing a letter to their neighbour anyway, when they could just as well walk over and visit in person. The post office is located at the airport because, quite frankly, most of the mail is sent by foreigners shipping packages out of the country.

Once I located the small counter at the airport that serves as the *correios,* I wandered inside to find a woman sleeping behind the counter. One post office in town, and it does not appear to get much business. I gently whistled a couple of times until the woman awoke. I proceeded to ask her if I could send a letter to Canada, and she quickly calculated the cost. About $5 to go half way around the world. Not bad. She then pulled a scrap of paper off a pile and ran it through an old postage machine that printed a stamp onto it. She searched for some scissors, cut the imprint out of the scrap of paper, and my letter was almost ready to mail. Using her thumb and forefinger, she extricated a Popsicle stick from a sticky, oozing jar and smeared glue onto the back of my stamp, and stuck it on the upper right hand corner of my envelope.

As she wiped the excess glue from my envelope, I paid her with a bill that was too large. She reached down and picked the plastic sack that served as a cash register up off the floor by her feet, put my bill inside, and fished out the proper change. The plastic sack strained under the weight of the coins it held—unusual in a culture that rarely has proper change.

The whole experience was fun and relaxed. The postal clerk was a lovely, friendly lady who apologized for having been sleeping. I may have been her first and last customer of the day. It seemed more like a social visit than a business transaction, which made for an overall positive, albeit unusual, experience. And the best news is that my packages arrived in less than two weeks. Chalk one up for the Mozambique postal service.

Christmas in July?

It cannot be December yet. It cannot be.

There is a strong wind blowing today, but not the usual Canadian crisp breeze coming down from Santa's workshop. It is more like the thick air blowing from the business end of a hairdryer.

It is hot outside. The kind of hot that requires two showers a day. Africa hot. And yet, Christmas is coming.

We unfolded a small artificial Christmas tree over the weekend. It has some garland and ornaments, but no lights. It is a sad little Charlie Brown sort of tree. But it reminds us that Christmas is coming, just as it reminded our apartment's previous tenants for Christmases past.

We are thankful for the Christmas CD that we received from friends back home. We will probably wear it out this year reminding ourselves that Christmas is coming.

How will I be sure Christmas has arrived if I do not even have to wear my wool hat when I go outside?

This is supposed to be the season of Advent. The season of anticipation and preparation for the coming of the baby Jesus. The

King Jesus. But at church on Sunday, there were no advent wreaths, no candles, no carols.

My usual prompts are conspicuously absent. The weather, the commercialism, even the religious symbols. Maybe this year we will be able to focus on preparing our hearts rather than our homes.

There is always something to distract us from the preparations of Advent. Sometimes it comes in the form of a packed shopping mall. (There is nothing that saps my patience like trying to park at a shopping mall on a Saturday in December!) For Martha, it comes in the form of the preparations themselves. The straightening, the tidying, the scrubbing. The incessancy. She was distracted by making everything just so.

For us this year, it will be the heat. And the distance of family. And yet, Christmas is coming. Jesus is coming.

By the People, for the People

We have started over the past days to have conversations with small groups of people about hiring them as "micro-enterprise development coordinators." These would be people who we could train in our remaining time here to organize communities into village-based savings and loan associations that will form the foundation of our business-development strategy. If I can recruit and train trainers before leaving, they can continue to implement this strategy long after I am gone.

These micro-enterprise development coordinators would be people from Mozambique who, because they do not have a cultural barrier to surmount, would be more effective trainers and mentors than I, a stranger, could ever be.

In our first such conversation, I was heartened that at least some of the people were catching our vision both for micro-enterprise development and for using Mozambicans as trainers.

Potholes, Padlocks and Poverty

"You guys see that Mozambicans have brains too," one of the meeting participants observed. "It usually seems like it is the white man to the rescue." I have to admit that, for a compliment, it stung a little. Sometimes people back home have difficulty seeing past the colour of others' skin; I should not expect anything different here.

The people we have spoken with have been unanimous in their enthusiasm for our vision.

Selecting the right people to hire to implement our vision promises to be an interesting challenge. The first issue that we have to deal with is trust: trust seems to be a commodity in short supply in Mozambique.

Employees are not used to being trusted. They are usually subjected to complex and bureaucratic structures that serve to emphasize this missing trust. Compensating for missing trust is the driving force behind the tangle of red tape that I observed at the hardware store shortly after we moved into our apartment and that is commonplace throughout the country.

And employees do not trust that employers will award jobs based on merit. In African culture, it is the responsibility of employers to wield their power in a way that benefits their family and friends. To do otherwise would be to neglect the needs of those closest to you.

That is an interesting twist on the nepotism debate, but it is clearly at work in Mozambique. RENAMO, Mozambique's opposition party, recently criticized the governing FRELIMO party over the lack of independence of the civil service. RENAMO claims that membership in the governing party is a prerequisite for government employment. Nonsense, was Luisa Diogo's reply. She is Mozambique's Prime Minister, and has responsibility of overseeing the independent body established to depoliticize the government's hiring practices.

What Ms. Diogo did not find important to mention in her rebuttal was that the head of this independent body is her sister, Victoria. "Is there nobody else in the entire country" qualified to run the civil service commission, the RENAMO questioner wondered aloud.

Nepotism and other unfair hiring practices are not restricted to the highest levels of government, either.

Yesterday, Timóteo shared with me the story of how he received his first job.

"I woke up in the morning and made a plan to knock on every door along Avenida 25 de Setembro," he recalled, referring to one of the major streets in Maputo. "After about three hours, I walked through a door and told the receptionist that I was looking for work, as I had for countless doors before. I told her that I was willing to do any work, it did not matter what the task was."

"Did you read the sign above the door on your way in?" she asked him.

"Yes, you are a security company."

"And you are a young boy. How old are you?"

"23."

"We do not hire anyone under 25. And we are looking for tall, strong men. You are too small. I am sorry, but we do not have anything for you here."

As Timóteo turned to walk out the door, he recalled sensing her attitude change. She saw something in me, he recalled, and took an interest in me. "Young man," she called to his back as he retreated toward the door, "let me make a phone call and see what I can do for you." She proceeded to pick up the phone and dialled the number to her boss. "I am here with my nephew," she said, "and he needs a job. His uncle has recently died, forcing him to move by himself to the city and...."

Potholes, Padlocks and Poverty

Timóteo's recollection of her exact story trailed off. It was not his story. He had no idea where she pulled it from. But after a visit with the boss, who at first phoned the secretary back insisting that she must be joking that this small boy could be useful as a security guard, Timóteo was offered his first job.

He recalls standing in a line of new recruits as the boss fastened shoulder patches to their new uniforms. One stripe was typical for the new recruits, and two for select individuals with driver's licenses. Timóteo, not measuring up to the other security guards but falsely believed to be family by the boss, was given three stripes—unheard of for new recruits. His job would be to supervise a team of these bigger, stronger guards lined up on either side of him.

In our own hiring practices, Glenn and I can try to combat these issues of trust by demonstrating as fair and open a recruitment process as possible and by creating systems that promote trust rather than suffocate it. But other challenges will remain, most notably putting people with little experience (remember that half the population is under 18 years old) or formal education (over half the population is illiterate, and few have had the privilege of completing high school) in charge of implementing the program. And determining a "fair" rate of pay in a developing country.

We are looking for people who are excited about our vision; people who will be excited to implement it. We are hoping that people do not come just for the promise of a secure job.

A Crisis of Conscience

I did something that is tearing me up inside. My heart is aching.

I made a decision based on the cold, calculated, compartmentalized budgeting rules that have been instilled in me since I was a young boy.

I told my Portuguese tutor that I did not have any more money for lessons.

I still have money to pay the rent, and I am not worried about having enough money for food.

I can still afford to drive my car.

I am not experiencing a financial meltdown.

It is just that the specific amount of money allocated for learning Portuguese has been exhausted. (Truth be known, it was probably exhausted a month ago, but I delayed the decision to stop my lessons because I just could not handle breaking the news to my tutor.)

Westerners hate to mix friendship and finances. It puts a bad taste in our mouths. The sincerity of friendship is suspect if it is tainted by monetary considerations. But Africans do not feel that way. Laura has tried to convince me that he will be grateful for the months of support I gave him, and that it is better to stop now— while we are still here, so I can help him bridge the gap in the coming months—rather than flying away, leaving him cold turkey, in June.

And she is probably right.

But I am still full of painful doubt. Hiring people is fun. Letting them go is definitely not.

Manna from Heaven

It was a race so secretive that even its participants were not aware of the plot. Their sponsors released their entry into the race and cheered, hoping that it would finish the course quickly.

But the race was unpredictable, and fraught with danger. It was the adult equivalent of little boys and girls racing their homemade stick rafts down a river, coaxing their rafts on from the sidelines, ever hopeful of victory, but in the end powerless to affect the outcome. Some fortunate rafts fared well. Others would be detoured by the spiralling flow of eddies; others, their fate much worse, would get stuck in a tangle of bushes along the shore or smashed against a rock.

Some of this race's sponsors expressed disappointment at hearing that they would not finish in first place. Some wondered if they would ever finish at all. It was, after all, a race half way around the globe.

To finish the race at all was a victory in itself.

Even the race marshals waiting at the finish line to crown the champion had no knowledge of which entry was nearing the finish line, or which entry was irretrievably lost. The victors of this race would appear suddenly, as if falling from the sky. Manna from heaven, the race marshals thought.

Having fallen from heaven, the manna landed in a post office box across the border in Nelspruit, South Africa. The parcels that have been arriving have contained useful gifts, entertaining gifts, and gifts that remind us of home. Our parents have sent gifts, our friends have sent gifts, and our small group from church has sent gifts. We have heard of other gifts having been sent, but they are probably stuck swirling in an eddy somewhere between Mississauga and Maputo. They may emerge yet.

We received some books to read, some games to play, and some television shows on DVD to watch. Otherwise, we only have Portuguese television.

Most of the household things that we would want can be found in Africa. Sure, most of the locals stick to the basic staples, but there is a large enough foreign and emerging wealth community that branded consumer goods are becoming available as well. General categories of food products are available, but often specific preferences are more difficult to satisfy. Milk is available, for instance, but fresh milk is a challenge. We buy aseptically sealed, boxed milk that has a shelf life, without refrigeration, that can be measured in months or years. Even the farm-fresh eggs are kept on shelves in the grocery store, non-refrigerated.

One of Canada's great myths—that eggs need to be refrigerated—has been shattered by Africans who have no choice but to store them on a hot shelf.

One lady wrote us an email from Oregon. She had not met us yet, but would be travelling to Mozambique and wondered if there was anything that she could bring that we could not buy in Africa. A wonderful gesture, we thought, and without too much consideration decided that what we wanted were cans of Campbell's condensed soups. Soup is available here, but most abundantly in powdered form, not cans of condensed liquid.

This kind lady from Oregon was amazed that the holidays could be brightened by such a simple gift. Her Christmas, she commented, would be shaped by these strangers she met in Mozambique who, when asked for anything, wanted only soup. (Okay, so we really like soup!)

All of the packages eventually arrived. The straggler award goes to a package mailed by my mother on November 7. It arrived on February 16. It was apparently stuck in postal office purgatory for over three months.

A Nation's Own Sons and Daughters

They have put it off, postponed it, re-scheduled it various times, but in the week before Christmas, I was finally scheduled to meet once again with the church leaders. Over six weeks have passed since I first encountered their spirited opposition. Then, as I was springing open the padlocks securing our front door, balancing an armload of bananas to bring with me to the meeting (since the oranges were such a hit last time), I received an SMS on my cell phone. The meeting was cancelled yet again.

Potholes, Padlocks and Poverty

With Christmas upon us, it will not be rescheduled until mid-January at the earliest. With Christmas also comes summer holidays, and I hear that little happens in Maputo for three or four weeks.

My heart sank.

Since my last meeting with these leaders, I have taken their concerns and shaped them into a strategy that I feel works for everyone, grounded by the village-based savings and loan program. I have sold it to our organization, to our board of directors, to supporters who will finance the project. I even had a conversation with a Mozambican elder who advises these church leaders. Wonderful, he said. Just what Mozambique needs.

Only I keep hitting my knees on this final hurdle. My attempts to sell the strategy to the leaders of the local churches has given me nothing but bruises layered on top of figurative bruises. Some on my knees, some on my ego.

I have not successfully separated this project from the broader politics of development work swirling around me. The leaders of the church, it seems, are holding this project hostage until we bring money to the table. There is no point teaching us about business if you do not give us money at the same time, they argue.

It is painful for those people who are used to receiving charity to suddenly be asked to provide their own resources. They doubt themselves and their own abilities. And some even think that we are bluffing: that eventually we will "cave in" and bring a truckload of money (your money—donor money—I might add). But that money would soon run out, leaving everyone in the same position as they are in today, and having dug the rut of dependency a little deeper.

They see us as being selfish and greedy for having money and not providing it. The perception prevails in Africa that money grows on trees in the West. (Comparatively speaking, that may even be true.)

Our revised strategy is based upon the belief that Mozambicans have within themselves and within their communities the resources to be successful on their own, without being dependent upon foreigners. The strategy is also built upon the principle that Mozambicans are best equipped to convince Mozambicans about the truth of this statement.

Yes, it can be harmful to give money. Jesus taught that money is poisonous. That is not to say that everyone who indulges succumbs. It is just a well-reasoned caution. And this particular group of church leaders is intoxicated.

Their intoxication is not representative of the whole of Africa. Right under my nose, I spoke with my good friend Mario, who is sobered to the reality of Africa. Sobered to the reality that Africans have all the resources that they need to survive and thrive. God has ensured this. He would not have made it any other way. *"Are not two sparrows sold for a penny?"* Jesus asks his disciples (in Matthew 10:29,31), *"Yet not one of them will fall to the ground apart from the will of your Father...So don't be afraid; you are worth more than many sparrows."*

Mario gave me much needed encouragement for insisting that Africans have the resources to help Africans. Africans need to take risks, he said, so that they can value their possessions. "If foreigners keep giving us things, we will never learn the value of money, or the value of hard work."

Mario's wisdom unleashed for me a compelling insight: if I really believe that Africans are best equipped and most credible to implement any development or evangelism work in Africa, then I ought to also believe that Africans are best equipped and most credible to convince Africans that such work is valuable and desirable in the first place.

The objective of our program is to identify and remove any barriers to economic development that exist for church and community members. I keep banging my knees against this hurdle because I myself am a barrier. My organizational affiliation, my affluence, my language, my culture, the colour of my skin. All of these factors reinforce one another to form an insurmountable, impenetrable barrier.

I am a barrier to the success of my own program because as long as I am the "front man," as long as it is me pitching the program, this group of church leaders will expect me to capitulate and bring money to the table. And they will prevent me from implementing the strategy until I do.

In order to stay true to our strategic vision, I must remove myself from the equation and allow Mozambican to interface directly with Mozambican. In order to achieve success, I must surrender a degree of control over, and credit for, the program.

God has laid down the gauntlet for me. You say you want My will to be done? Are you willing to step aside from this project? Are you willing to withdraw your ego from this project in order for My will to be realized?

In order to stay true to God's calling, I must remove myself from the front lines.

God never promises that His call will be easy, but to step back from my own project is a challenge. Wow.

My work will move upstream, with me in a less visible, less central role. And the role that Glenn and I had envisioned for the program coordinators that we are recruiting will expand as a result. When I return from holidays, the task will change from trying to get airtime with the committee of leaders directly in order to sell the need for the strategy, to supporting, encouraging and equipping people like Mario to sell the strategy to his nation's own sons and daughters.

Like Martha, We Were Busy Preparing

Despite our best intentions, we did not make it to a Christmas church service this year. Instead, we were inescapably snared in the African time trap. A trap that Martha knows all too well.

The trap was set a couple of days ago by Mario, who was talking about his church's plans for an evening Christmas service followed by a social time. We do not have enough time to sit around and get to know one another, he said, and was really looking forward to creating such an opportunity this Christmas.

We offered our kitchen for Mario, his brother Dilson, and their cousin to come prepare some Christmas snacks. It would take two hours, they said, or three, tops. They arrived shortly after noon, and for hours we mixed, rolled, and deep-fried samosas (or *xamussas,* as they call them), spring rolls, chicken, French fries, and hamburgers (yes, even the hamburgers were deep fried). Anything not deep-fried was smothered in mayonnaise.

Eight hours later, "some Christmas snacks" were finished, with a feast sufficient to feed the entire church of 40 people.

As we made the preparations, Laura battled to keep anything with meat or mayonnaise in the fridge. It was a cultural battle; a gargantuan battle between the fridge-people and the non-fridge people (the importance of keeping food in the fridge is lost on people who do not have electricity in their homes). The battle ended in a draw.

My battle was more of an internal fight: an epic struggle to maintain bodily hydration. Our house, lacking air conditioning, strains under the weight of the African heat at the best of times; having the oven and several stove elements pumping additional heat into our cramped kitchen for hours made me crave running outside to roll in the Canadian Christmastime snow.

We can dream all we want. The snow is not coming for Christmas.

Maputo was experiencing a communist-style run on soft drinks, forcing me to wait half an hour in the beating-down sun to exchange a crate of empties before the party. I fared better than Melvin, who was told that stores had run out of Coca-Cola and Pineapple Fanta.

The time trap tightened, with the tick-tick-tick of the clock growing louder and louder as the kitchen became hotter and hotter.

After eight hours of sweating at the vegetable market, in the line up for soft drinks, and in the kitchen, we were finished making the feast that would feed an entire church. Just in time, too: now past 8pm, the church had started their evening program two hours earlier. We loaded up the car and drove slowly to the church, weaving around potholes like we were in a battleground minefield, plates and platters of food balanced precariously in the passengers' hands, laps, and any other mostly flat surface that could be found in the car.

The great virtue of the African time trap is that few people cared that we were so late, and even those few who did had their cares melt away at the sight of the feast. And an hour after we arrived, the evidence of our labour was reduced to crumbs on plates and smiles on faces.

Merry Christmas!

A Season of Change

Christmas has come and gone for another year, and now it is that time when people attempt to reorder their lives by making New Year's resolutions. Time for change.

In Mozambique, this really is a season of change, but not for the reasons you might expect. No, there is a different sort of change afoot. Here, there is an important game of hot potato under way, stemming from the government's decision to strip three zeros from its currency. The 1,000,000 meticais bill has been replaced by its successor, the 1,000. Each dollar is now equivalent to 25 meticais nova familia—the "new family"—not 25,000.

Mozambicans have until December 31 to get rid of their old bills. By the time the calendar year rolls over, we face the hassle of exchanging them at the government's central bank. Possible, but a hassle.

And the game is heating up. The new bills were introduced several months ago, but I have received more of the old ones in the past couple of weeks than over the past months combined. They are withered, tattered, filthy bills. Especially the small ones. And they are hot.

There is another interesting phenomenon about change: apparently, in Africa, it is the responsibility of the person making the purchase to have the necessary change. Stores, particularly small ones, do not have much. Here, the equivalent of a $20 bill is too large for all but the biggest stores. The cashier's glare frequently burns a hole through even my bills worth eight dollars. In Africa, such "large" bills are argentum non gratae.

Because of this phenomenon, I recently paid $2 too much for a $15 refill on a propane tank. It was either that or no gas. The salesman did not have change.

And I am routinely asked by merchants for change so that they can settle up with customers ahead of me in line.

I guess in this way, it is the season of "no change," unless the merchant happens to have a hot potato that needs to be passed along. Happy New Year!

Now, Unlock Your Own Mission Field

1. Read Luke 10:38-42. What concrete actions can you take—or avoid—in order to live like Mary in a world dominated by Marthas?

Challenge Yourself:

Identify a missionary (through your church or by contacting a missionary organization—they will have many suggestions) and send them a simple gift from home. Include a personal note. It may take a long time to show up, but it will be appreciated when it does.

7 Smelling Africa's Beautiful Flowers

The Many Contrasts of Cape Town

There are plenty of places on this continent and in this country that experience greater poverty than urban Maputo. There are certainly a few wealthier places, as well. Nowhere are these contrasts as sharp as in South Africa, and perhaps nowhere in South Africa are they as distinct as in Cape Town, where we spent some holiday time this month.

Cape Town is a city of wealth unknown in Maputo, even if that wealth is only a thinly brushed veneer. Travelling from the airport, we passed entire neighbourhoods of Africa's trademark corrugated tin roof shanties and plenty of evidence of more solidly built but equally small housing provided by the government. The seeds of progress. Cape Town's poverty was quickly left behind as we reached the office towers and tourist shops that make up the city bowl.

Cape Town is the legislative capital of South Africa. It is the city where Nelson Mandela was imprisoned on Robben Island in the height of the country's disgrace called apartheid, and where he later took his seat as the post-apartheid republic's first president. Immediately beside the seat of legislative power is a museum that was once a slave lodge prominent in a city that served as an important hub of slave trade activity. The museum that now celebrates racial freedom

109

creates parallels between South Africa's apartheid experience and the Civil Rights movement in the United States, drawing inspiration from the latter that South Africa can move beyond its racist history.

Simo, who lives 2,700 kilometres away in Malawi but works in Cape Town part of each year to earn much-needed money, was our host at a small bed and breakfast that we used as our staging ground as we prepared our day-long excursions into the city. He preferred home: sure, Cape Town is beautiful, but the problem is that it is on the ocean. When people have no money, they have nowhere to go for fresh water. At least people in Malawi, situated on a large inland freshwater lake, do not die of hunger, he said.

The fact is that people in Malawi die far too frequently of starvation, but Simo's point was that there are certain benefits to being able to live in a country where survival does not depend on participation in a formal trade-based economy. Simo's life back home, where the lakes are full of fresh water and the neighbourhood trees shed plentiful fruit for the taking, is free of the complexities of a global world.

We met another man who also lives in Malawi but works in Cape Town's booming tourism industry to be able to send money home. Working as a hotel porter is far better than the harsh conditions faced by the previous generation, he thought, who travelled to South Africa to earn money working in the gold mines of Johannesburg.

Cape Town continued to build upon our image of Africa as a continent of natural beauty, as well, and in so doing drove the stake deeper into the heart of the mythology of Africa as a dry, desolate, and depressing desert.

Who, Us? Unwelcome?

As comfortable as we have become in Africa, it is useful for us to remember that the country whose name is printed on the front of our passports is our home. Everywhere else, we are just visitors.

Everywhere else, we are just guests who can be asked to leave.

Part of our vacation in Cape Town was spent plumbing the ranks of South Africa's Department of Home Affairs, trying to seek permission to stay in the country long enough to finish our seven days of holidays.

The problem started quietly in September with a border official who neglected to stamp our passport on our way out of South Africa. And then, just as quietly, another forgot to stamp it on the way back in six weeks later. Because of the missing stamps, it looked to the border guard on our most recent entry that we had overstayed our welcome in South Africa on our previous visit. We would still be allowed in the country, but we had to speak with someone at Home Affairs. And just to be sure that we would, he scribbled instructions to that effect across our visa in our passports.

This note was written at Jeppe's Reef, between Swaziland and South Africa. We had the first several days booked in Kruger Park. After that stay, the ink on the notation dried a little further as we travelled to Cape Town, and further still as the government offices closed early on Friday and sat locked up over the weekend.

The day before we were set to become illegal in South Africa, we finally found our way into Home Affairs and were received by a lady with a long list of requirements to fulfill: we can fix this problem for you, but first you will have to have proof of your plans to exit the country (difficult when we arrived in a private car, but parked it at an airport hundreds of kilometres away), proof of sufficient funds to finance our stay (difficult since we have no bank account in Africa), and pay R425 each as an application fee and R2200 as a security deposit, refundable once we leave the country.

We scrambled to assemble these things, and returned the next morning to speak to a new person behind the counter. This new person, a man, was friendlier but after several hours had only bad news: unfortunately, our application was denied, and there was nothing he could do. He had even checked with his colleague, who agreed that the visa could not be extended. We had to leave the country that day. No matter that Maputo is 1,600 kilometres away, and no matter that we had no way to travel that distance.

Luckily, the man was friendly despite his no-nonsense message. He pulled out a scrap piece of paper and started diagramming for us why we were unwelcome in his country. The missing stamps in our passports fabricated a story that we were living in South Africa, staying from temporary visa to temporary visa, leaving only long enough to have a new visa issued. He was sympathetic enough to my corrected version of our situation that he was willing to let us speak to his boss, though he initially thought even this to be futile: "It will be difficult to assemble the machinery of management to get this approved in a single day," he breathed on our way out.

We found his boss upstairs, a busy bureaucrat who found importance in being seen to run from task to task. "If you try to chase two rabbits," he counselled us, fretting among the stacks of paper burying his desk, "you are not likely to catch either one." He proceeded to shake his head and wonder why he could not heed his own advice. I tried to gain his sympathy by commenting that he appeared to be chasing at least a dozen.

He listened to our story, and made a note on a scrap of paper for us to bring downstairs to the man at the counter. His penmanship was the calibre of an important doctor, and it seemed that his prescription must have been for us to wait in line for several more hours.

Back downstairs, the friendly man at the counter stapled this note to our paperwork and passed the file to the next bureaucrat to process, who also sent it up to Mr. Fudd, the wabbit hunter, to approve our "unique case." After an hour of silence, we ventured back upstairs. By evidence of banging his fist against the plasterboard office partitions, Mr. Fudd's day was not improving, but he too was surprisingly friendly and helpful. Our paperwork was found within a foot-thick pile to be processed whenever time permitted, but he pulled it out, wrote another prescription, and sent us back downstairs.

Within 30 minutes we had new visas allowing us to stay in South Africa until April if we so desired, and without having to pay a penny for the permit. It turns out that we were, once again, welcome to stay.

A Fresh Coat of Paint and Some Dynamite

Cape Town is a beautiful city, a wealthy city. If it were ripped from its African roots and floated across to the other side of the Atlantic, it would fit in without much trouble amongst the cities of North America. It is not without crime and poverty, but it also has a feeling of promise and hope.

I have heard repeatedly that, 30 years ago, there were many African capitals in this same situation. Maputo, the evidence would show, was among these.

Jeffrey Sachs, in his insightfully and optimistically written bestseller, *The End of Poverty*, backs my anecdotal evidence with hard data: sub-Saharan Africa has increased in both the absolute number and proportion of population living in extreme poverty over the 20-year period of 1981 to 2001. Africans have, on average, become poorer over the past quarter century.

The core of Maputo consists of high- and low-rise buildings built with typically ornate Portuguese architecture along wide, Jacaranda-lined avenues. It whispers secrets about a long-past beauty, but today many of its buildings are crumbling.

The towering Four Seasons hotel reveals some of Maputo's

113

worst-kept secrets. From a distance, it is a hotel that stands as a proud beacon on the shores of the Indian Ocean. Surely it has entertained scores of the world's wealthy and famous. It does not take a keen observer to notice, however, that the hotel has never hosted a single guest. Its unfinished concrete frame stands as a beacon of distrust, not pride. This distrust resulted in policies such as the infamous "24-20" edicts at the end of the revolution, by which the minister of the interior (and now current president), Armando Guebuza, evicted any white resident suspected of being a counter-revolutionary. Guebuza's edict gave such suspects, without so much as a trial or opportunity for defence, 24 hours to leave the country and restricted them to 20 kilograms of luggage each.

The Portuguese fled, leaving the civil service and most businesses without a sufficient number of trained employees to allow for a successful transition of power. The Four Seasons hotel was left unfinished, and rumours have circulated for the subsequent three decades about saboteurs having poured cement down the elevator shafts and through the plumbing; rumours that the Portuguese architects had fled with the drawings.

It is nothing but an empty, vacant, abandoned shell, and has never been anything but an empty shell. And behind the shell is a massive crater serving as a reminder that, during the floods of March 2000, hundreds of homes and countless lives in the Maputo suburb of Polana Caniço were washed out into the ocean.

There has been a long line of companies that have attempted to complete or redevelop the hotel, but for 30 years, company after company has walked away and the rumours of sabotage have persisted. The latest proposal is that the US government is going to implode the building in February to make room for a new ocean-front embassy and residential compound.

If these plans come to fruition, the disappearance of this blight will represent for some Mozambicans another step along the cathartic path to reconstruction. And for countless others, its implosion will have no greater impact than providing an afternoon of cheap entertainment.

Alzira, Empregada

Mozambique, unsurprisingly, is characterized by low labour costs. Because costs are so low, most everything is done manually. Here, for example, we have witnessed lines as they are painted on roads by a guy with a big brush and a can of paint. The street sweeper is literally a lady armed with a handmade broom as traffic charts a course dangerously close.

Because of the low labour costs, many middle- and upper-class residents of Mozambique can afford guards and cleaners for their homes. Alzira is the empregada (which translates simply as "worker") that we inherited with our apartment to come and clean it once a week.

We feel guilty being missionaries with a maid, but feel even worse at the thought of letting her go. Alzira's husband died less than a month before we arrived, leaving her to tend her children by herself. She is only able to find work twice a week, so we decided to keep using her to provide her with much-needed income, though we appreciate the help cleaning as well.

Her wage is 140 meticais (about $5.75) per day, a raise of $1 over her previous employers. Combined with another part-time job that Alzira has, her weekly income is about $10. We also pay her an extra 10 meticais for her transportation to and from work.

We decided that if she was going to work for us, we would like to visit her home and see how she lives, too. And once we were there, we knew that it was the right decision. The shy and reserved Alzira who avoids making eye contact in our apartment vanished. In her place was a broadly smiling Alzira who was proud to show us her home and her children.

She lives in a simple house, the entire yard being perhaps 1,000 square feet. The main building is a brick structure where the "living" is done (mostly sleeping, really). There is also a kitchen at the front of the property, strung together with spare materials, and a hole in the backyard where she is slowly building a washroom with money that she saves.

I thought that it must be strange having a kitchen and a washroom outside the house, but learned that many Mozambicans think we are just as strange for wanting them inside. Most cooking is done over open fires (of wood or charcoal), or with gas for those who can afford it. Keeping the kitchen outside reduces the pollutants in the house where the family sleeps. As well, not having to endure winter months means that "outside" and "inside" are boundaries that get blurred. Alzira's kitchen and washroom are just as close to her bedroom as are ours; the major difference is that our hallway happens to be covered by a roof, whereas hers is not. And her family can use the kitchen and bathroom before being able to save enough money to build a structure around them. Cooking is done in a fire pit beside the house before the walls of a kitchen are built around it. In Africa, homes are built in phases.

And, of course, because everything is done by hand in Mozambique, Alzira conducts these construction projects on her own. Her form of savings is very typical: when she has extra money, she buys building materials. She will continue building once she has accumulated enough material.

Yes, Math Is Important!

I had the opportunity of acting as a "quantity surveyor" on our post-secondary school construction project. Melvin asked me to measure the amount of work that the tile-setters had completed to ensure that they receive the correct payment.

If they receive too much, especially in Mozambique, they would still ask for payment when the work was actually done. Africans seem to have short memories, especially when they are on the winning side of a financial transaction, so it is important to not pay in advance.

We have some contracts in this situation. Some workers have received more money than they should have for the amount of work done to date, and the result is foot-dragging for the rest of the project. Having already been paid, they have had little incentive to work for months.

That cultural reality is perhaps at the heart of a World Bank report that recently re-affirmed sub-Saharan Africa's standing as the most difficult region in the world to do business. Amongst these countries, Mozambique is no exception as it continues to experience the pains of emerging from its post-independence days as a single-party socialist state.

On this day, the tile-setters were requesting payment for their work. Their contract stipulates that they be paid in three equal instalments over the course of the project, but with roughly two thirds of the work having been completed, they were asking for their tenth payment.

I calculated the value of the work done to date. Melvin, the site supervisor, calculated how much money they had received to date. The balance owing was a meagre $8 to be split amongst the entire team.

"Math is important," the trade supervisor told me, exasperated that he was owed so little. "I asked for an advance here and an advance there. I did not know it would add up to so much!" It became apparent that he had not been keeping records of money received.

Os Emprestimos

When I started learning Portuguese, I learned the word for "loan." *Emprestimo.* I thought that it would be a useful word to know when dealing with microcredit and business development. I did not realize how often I would hear it from individuals asking me for a loan. Queria um emprestimo, por favor.

Of course, the request is never that direct. Not in Africa.

We have been asked for many loans or gifts (the lines are rarely so clear) over the past months. Most recently it was Alzira, our empregada who asked for a loan. The conversation went something like this:

"Good morning, patron. How are you?"

"Good morning, Alzira. I am doing fine, thanks. How are you doing today?"

"I am fine as well. Laura is at school today?"

"Yes, she is at school."

"My mother is sick right now, but she is in Chokwe and I do not have enough money to visit her."

"I am sorry to hear that."

(And there it was, as simple as that. I directly responded to the explicit statement, not even detecting a request for a loan buried in there!)

I had inadvertently forced her to ask more directly:

"Could I have a loan for two hundred meticais so that I can travel there this weekend?" She felt embarrassed—her face clearly betrayed her sentiment—for having to be so direct, a clear indication that having the money was more important to her than being comfortable.

Some people have advised us against lending money to Mozambicans. Their reasons vary. Some people think that when Africans ask for a loan, they really have little intention of repaying it. In this case, if she had have asked for the $8 outright to visit her sick mother in a different province, I probably would have obliged.

Some people argue that we are not doing anyone any favours by helping them to live above their means. I am sympathetic to this point, but I am also sympathetic to her sick mother. And I would rather let her make a bad decision about her life than force my own decisions onto her.

In a perfect world, Africans would save their money so that they had some left over for a rainy day (or perhaps a more apt metaphor would be for a drought). In a perfect world, they would have enough to eat every day as well.

I can give her a loan because I can secure it against her future wages—after all, those wages come from my wallet. But that is not the point. The point is that we have a cultural bias towards savings, in part stemming from the comfort that comes from a stable political and economic climate.

Africans have had too turbulent a history to be able to count on their savings having any value tomorrow.

Instead, African culture permits the borrower, not the lender, to determine the level and legitimacy of their request. In some ways, that is a freeing thought. At least this time, I will not worry about whether or not I am helping or hurting.

A Culture Lost

A couple of years ago, Mel Lastman, the outspoken mayor of Toronto, embarrassed himself and our city with a demonstration of his lack of knowledge about Africa. On the eve of travelling to Mombasa Hamisi Mboga, Kenya, Mr. Lastman joked with reporters that he feared being hoisted into a vat of boiling water while natives danced around him.

He was preparing to travel to Kenya to promote Toronto's 2008 Olympic bid. The remark did not help our city's chances to win the Olympic Games and vault itself onto the international stage, and the Olympics were eventually awarded to Beijing.

(Yes, there are infrequent reports of cannibalism in Africa. There was also a case in Germany in 2001.)

Potholes, Padlocks and Poverty

Fears of boiling pots of cannibal soup aside, the tragic reality is that much African culture, like much native culture in North America, has been lost in large measure because of historic ignorance not unlike that exhibited by Mr. Lastman in Toronto.

Traditional tribal languages have also been pushed aside in favour of European languages. Mozambicans sometimes refer to their tribal languages not as languages, but more disparagingly as mere dialects. These are not real languages, their colonizers taught them, they are monkey languages.

Laura and I recently had the opportunity to visit a cultural village established to celebrate the heritage of the Shangana tribe, which is the predominant tribe in southern Mozambique. We witnessed traditional clothing and dance and partook in a traditional meal. The meal, as it turns out, was very similar to the one that we experienced at Paulo and Olga's wedding. Traditional food, it seems, has not been lost.

The most significant difference was the wedding's lack of traditional appetizers: worms, crocodile, and impala. These delicacies were not in short supply at the cultural village.

The very fact that we had to travel to a living museum to witness the traditional culture of the people in whose land we are immersed is telling. Today, many Mozambicans (particularly men) have shed traditional African flamboyancy in favour of the standard uniform of Westerners' clothing: pants and a shirt.

In some places, this is because of used clothing arriving courtesy of Westerners' donations. Evidence of this is common. People have no inhibitions about wearing t-shirts with tourist slogans scrawled across their chests, or sweatshirts advertising some little-known college in the United States, or someone's long-forgotten amateur softball uniform.

In Africa, a shirt is often just a shirt.

But this does not paint an accurate picture. Many Africans in

Mozambique wear clean and well-pressed clothing. Tasteful clothing. But not traditional African clothing. Their colonizers taught them to wear Western clothing.

Men do not wear *capulanas* anymore. Civilized men do not wear skirts.

Contempt for the culture practiced by the majority population of the derisively named Dark Continent was widespread among colonizers. Ian Smith, the last European Prime Minister of Rhodesia (now Zimbabwe), demonstrates this contempt in unapologetic fashion in his 1997 memoirs:

> *It is difficult for people who have never lived in this part of the world to appreciate that sub-Saharan Africa is different. It was the last part of our world to come into contact with western European civilization... The wheel had not even evolved, nor had the plough. The change which has taken place is absolutely phenomenal, and is a tribute to what the white inhabitants did over a period of ninety years.*[4]

The colonialists and the naive, it would seem, saw native Africans as monkeys in the jungle needing to be modernized. Or exploited.

It is shameful that so much of African culture has been lost.

And it is a shame that Africa must battle its image as a continent where visitors will be encountered at the airport by a throng of salivating cannibals dancing in their leopard-skin loincloths.

A Day at the Beach

It may be the bleak mid-winter back home, but not in Africa. On Saturday, our colleagues invited us to the beach at Marracuene. What a great way to see a bit more of Mozambique and relax at the

---

[4] Smith, *The Great Betrayal*, p. 55.

same time. Mozambique hugs the coast of the Indian Ocean and is reputed to have great beaches.

Of course, since Maputo is a port city, it is right on the ocean, but the locals tell us that the beaches are better a couple of kilometres out of the city.

Foreigners have advised us that the beaches are best a couple of hours beyond the city.

As it turns out, getting to the Marracuene beach is no picnic.

First, there was the ferry, they said. When we arrived at the docks, someone pointed to the ferry. I laughed, not for a second taking her seriously. That is clearly a raft, and a sketchy one at that. Before I had a chance to ask when the ferry would arrive, the man on the rickety little raft waived our truck on board.

Our truck barely fit, with our wheels hanging over the edge, but that seemed to concern only two passengers: Laura and myself.

I could not help but think that they would probably keep shuttling cars across the channel until the day the ferry sank. And wondered when the last time the safety inspector had come to visit. They do have safety inspectors, right?

After the short ferry ride, we had to drive along a road for about 45 minutes. Again, "road" was a poor choice of words. Between dodging small craters and herds of cattle, we likely would have been better off driving in the fields beside the road. Which, at some particularly rough points, our colleague Nate actually did.

Then we got to the sandy stretch, which reminded me of the morning after an all-night snowstorm in Canada, before the snowploughs had had a chance to clear the streets.

We eventually arrived intact, and the beach was magnificent. Given the journey, it should not have come as a big surprise that the beach was empty. We had it all to ourselves. Just us and our colleagues. And those little crabs playing in the surf, allowing themselves to get swept up in the warm salty water and riding it down again, as if at an amusement park.

Many people tend to think of Africa as a poor, dry, starving continent. Even a war-torn continent. But it is also a lovely continent, with much natural beauty to boast.

Now, Unlock Your Own Mission Field

1. What caricature of Africa do you have? What information sources have you used to build this caricature? Are they reliable? Accurate? Complete? What could you do to broaden this caricature?

Challenge Yourself:

Next time someone asks you for financial assistance—a friend, a homeless man on the street—try allowing them to be the judge of their need. They likely know you as well as you know them. Give them the benefit of the doubt. Trust that they need your help.

8 Gaining Some Traction, Finally

What is Poverty, Anyway?

Thinking about coming back to Canada, people have asked us how we can possibly integrate our new experiences of poverty with what we see back home. Can we have compassion for Canada's poor, many of whom benefit from a comparatively buoyant social safety net? Or should we focus all of our attention overseas?

My dad asked the question most directly: "We seem so disconnected in Canada that we cannot relate to the poor. I guess looking at us from where you are, there are no poor people in Canada." My dad's comment was in reaction to our observation of the poorest of the poor—the men and women who scavenge the garbage dumpsters looking for their small piece of survival.

On one level, he is right. There are few people in Canada who have so little in life that they are forced to find survival in the trash cast off by the world's poor. And yet, there are countless people in Canada who have less than nothing; whose debts outweigh their assets. Countless people who owe more than they have. Countless people who have to choose between paying the rent and buying groceries each month.

Even those waist deep in refuge inside of Maputo's dumpsters owe the world little, if only because the world trusts them with little.

Potholes, Padlocks and Poverty

But what does this say about poverty? What is poverty, if it cannot be calculated by an objective balancing of a personal ledger?

Perhaps one answer is that poverty is a lack of power; the solution, then, becomes giving the impoverished a sense of controlling her own destiny.

Money, after all, is nothing but a proxy for power.

Is a man without bread to eat, who lacks the power to control his own diet, considered poor? Most people would agree that he is.

What about the child forced to work in the squalid conditions of a sewing sweatshop until her fingers are numb, lacking the power to play with a ball in the courtyard, lacking the power to be a child? Again, little disagreement.

Or a young adult without a sufficient education, who lacks the power to land a steady job?

What about the immigrant who, having arrived in North America, realizes that his credentials are not recognized and is forced to drive a taxi in order to pay the rent? Sure, he keeps his family above water, but just barely.

Any development program, any intervention, any desire or action to help the poor should first be processed through this sieve: how is what I am proposing going to empower the poor? Will they be able to continue helping themselves long after I am gone or once the attention of the development community has been diverted to the next crisis?

Staring poverty in the eye in Mozambique, I wrestle often to understand which position is more enviable: being a generally happy person with few economic resources, or a wealthy person who feels enslaved by circumstances and expectations.

One of the most refreshing and surprising truths about Mozambique is that so many of the people here, who would fit squarely within most traditional definitions of poverty, are content. Life is not perfect for these people, but they are happy. They are in control of their lives, wear clean clothes, and are relatively healthy.

There are countless others who are extremely poor, who do not have enough to eat, or cannot afford medications when they are ill, or cannot afford to clothe their children in the uniforms that the school officials require. But perhaps these people are facing such dire circumstances not simply because they lack material wealth, but rather because they lack the ability to control their own destinies.

Those who are desperately poor may need help stepping onto the first rung of the development ladder, but this hand up must be given in a way that preserves or bolsters their sense of self-control and empowerment. To give someone material wealth but rob them of their self-worth is no gift at all. We will always feel poor, whether in Africa or America, as long as we believe that we are trapped by our circumstances, however real or imagined.

Olga's Frayed Nerves

I was reflecting this week on a question that I asked myself back in July. Before setting foot in Mozambique, I wondered what remnants I would find of a protracted civil war that has certainly, I thought, left some emotional and physical scars on this country and its people.

This week, I heard a story involving Olga, whose wedding we were at in the fall, that reveals an interesting example of the frayed nerves with which some people still struggle. Last Sunday, Olga was injured and briefly hospitalized in what she believed was the resumption of the country's once-protracted and bloody civil war, which ended with a ceasefire in 1992.

She was not wounded by fighting; instead, her injuries were sustained as she jumped out of the window of the minibus taxi that she was riding in when she heard the eruption of explosions and gunfire. Fearing for her life, she desperately wanted to flee.

As it turns out, she need not have been alarmed. The country is still at peace, but ringing in her ears were the haunting noises of the civil war era: for 45 minutes on Sunday afternoon, obsolete mortar shells and other military equipment exploded in a fire apparently started by the heat of the African summer.

The scars of battle are deep. And for some people, like Olga, fear simmers just below the surface.

The Price of the Church

A knock came at our door this morning from Samuel, one of the men to whom Glenn and I offered a job as a coordinator of our micro-enterprise development program. He stopped by to discuss some of the position's details.

Salary, it turns out, is a sticking point.

Some Mozambicans have an expression for jobs that do not pay very well. They pay the price of the banana. Bananas are cheap and so, I presume, are those employers.

There is a lesser-known expression, too. The price of the church. Apparently in the grand hierarchy of employment, the church is even cheaper than the banana.

It is that way for good reason. People are supposed to work for the church not for the promise of riches, but because they have a passion for the work. They accept such jobs because they feel a calling from God and willingly accept the sacrifice.

Sure, my conscience says, but that cannot become an excuse for the church to abuse its employees, especially when the purpose of our program is to develop Mozambicans' economic well-being to ensure that hunger and illness are distant memories. Besides, we want to allow the coordinators of our program sufficient time and motivation to operate their own micro-enterprises, like Samuel's barbershop, so that they are received as credible, knowledgeable micro-enterprise trainers. We also do not want to cut them off from all other economic activity, knowing that this year's salary is backed by a promise and next year's is backed by a hope. Nothing, until we have sufficient money in the bank, can be backed by a guarantee. That is the nature of fundraising.

So what is a fair salary in a third-world country? We are offering a salary of 2,500 meticais—or a little under $100—a month, which is, apparently, the price of the church. I do not have access to a proper salary survey to benchmark against, but I do know what some others are paying. I have only enough information to know that we are offering neither the highest nor the lowest of salaries.

And we are offering a high enough salary that nobody ever quotes it in the context of defining the poor. Extreme poverty is usually defined to be those people who earn something less than $1 per day. Half of the world, the same sources usually quote, live on less than $2 per day.

At $100 a month—$3.29 a day—our salary is, according to Samuel, higher than what entry-level government jobs are paying in Maputo. And, to be clear, Samuel was not arguing for a ten-fold increase, but a ten- or twenty-percent increase, not unlike anyone at home trying to squeeze out a slightly higher salary.

I have no illusions that this salary is anyone's idea of a get-rich-quick scheme, but it is not going to leave anyone in Africa hungry or homeless, either.

Of course, I do not mean to suggest that I approached the conversation in cavalier fashion. What moral footing do I have to argue the sufficiency of this wage with the man sitting across the table from me in my $650 per month apartment? Looking through my lens, I have made a huge sacrifice to live in Mozambique. To him, I am still a king, albeit perhaps one who relinquished a crown jewel or two. How can I look Samuel in the eye and argue that $100 a month is a good salary?

Potholes, Padlocks and Poverty

I have just closed the door behind my guest, and I am feeling emotionally spent. I am feeling a little bruised and beaten, not because Samuel was even remotely abusive or impolite. The bruises have been inflicted by my own conscience, battling the merits of offering a salary the size of which, I admitted to Samuel, would leave me starving to death.

The Incredible Shrinking Globe

Maputo used to be 13,700 kilometres from our home in Mississauga. Now, it seems, it is just another suburb.

How do I know this? Laura telephoned her grandmother. Granddaughter using a laptop, internet connection, and Skype software; grandmother using a standard old telephone plugged into her wall and serviced by Ma Bell, just like it has been for decades. Laura's grandmother could not quite understand how she seemed so close. "When your grandfather went off to war," she said, "I was not able to talk to him for four years." Needless to say, both were happy for this new world.

The short commute between Mississauga and Maputo provides an important lesson about poverty as well. I learned this lesson when my friend Mario stopped in at our house today. You know, two-dollar-a-day Mario. No electricity or running water Mario. No roof over his head Mario.

I offer him something to eat almost every time he comes, and on occasion, when he is really hungry, he accepts. He will always accept a glass of water, but preferably not straight out of the fridge.

Today, Mario wanted to ask me for a favour. No problem, I thought. What kind of favour would he ask, I wondered. Probably a loan, I thought.

"Could I please use your computer to check my Gmail account?" Wow, I thought. Gmail in Africa.

And while he was checking his Gmail account, I helped him read a piece of junk mail that he received. "Could it really be true that I have won $500,000 and a new Toyota car?" he asked me. We were both in awe; he, because he saw a sliver of possibility that riches had been heaped on this poor man by some unknown source. Me, because this poor man receives electronic junk mail despite not having electricity in his home.

Wow. Even Africa's poor receive spam.

I argued earlier that poverty is the antonym of power, that the solution to poverty is not wealth, but empowerment. First, clean drinking water, some bread, maybe even some basic medicines, and then empowerment. A sense of controlling one's own destiny.

Technology has empowered two-dollar-a-day Mario with global knowledge. New tools built on top of a platform of technology mean that I have been able to have intelligent conversation with an undereducated, impoverished African about weapons of mass destruction, the retirement of Kofi Annan and the value of the UN in global diplomacy, and the death penalty in places like California and Florida.

It sounds strange, but travelling to Africa felt like coming to a new world, not unlike the Portuguese explorers who colonized Mozambique. Now that I have been here for half a year, I have realized that the globe has shrunk a lot in the last half-millennium. It has shrunk so much that Mario, who is my neighbour now, will continue to be once I have moved back to Canada, as well. Maputo has become a suburb of Mississauga.

Set Up for Success

Great news. We have hired Samuel and Mario as two micro-enterprise development coordinators. Both agreed to work for a salary of $100 per month. Now the real challenge begins: equipping these two men who have demonstrated a passion and willingness to help their fellow Mozambicans to develop and implement a successful program.

Glenn and I both leave in a little under four months, and we cannot help but hear a loud ticking sound in our ears as the time grows closer and closer.

One of the things that we are particularly mindful of is to start out with these new coordinators firmly holding the torch of responsibility for this new program. For the next four months, we will walk alongside them to help and encourage, but the torch is in their hands.

The torch analogy is borrowed from a mentor who once described evangelism and development projects this way: he said that his experience has shown him that good programs often fail as the foreign creators of the program attempt to pass the torch to national leadership. The torch, he cautioned, is often dropped in the transfer.

Great programs avoid this pitfall by starting out with the torch firmly in the hands of nationals who can provide consistent, local leadership to the program. The nationals own the vision for the program from the outset.

Great words, but what do they mean in practice? That is our present challenge.

Barriers to success—the weak points where leaders stumble and risk dropping the torch—come in all shapes and sizes. We are working hard to identify and avoid as many as possible.

When we leave, these coordinators will be required to carry out the program without the benefit of our cars, so for the next four months, Glenn and I will avoid shuttling them around in our cars. Walking or taking local transit will be less efficient, but will prevent creating a barrier to continuity that would need to be torn down later.

If the coordinators need to send an email, they will use an internet café.

If they need to make a presentation, they will do so using materials and resources available to them, not our laptops and projectors.

Past programs have failed to transition to national leadership for the simplest of reasons. I have had it explained to me, for example, that a Mozambican could not continue a training program that a missionary had previously started because that missionary had handed out certificates at its completion (something that we had done earlier as well). The program needed certificates in order to be legitimate, the Mozambican reasoned, but he did not have the means of making any.

Certificates may be nice, but that is a lousy reason to not continue a program. Certificates, unless they can be produced locally, are a barrier to sustainability that we need not create.

Reflecting on sustainability when I first arrived, I thought that I would act only where absolutely necessary as an up-front leader. Almost half a year later, I have not found any situation in which it has been absolutely necessary for me to lead by standing in front of a group. The only reason I have found to do so is for my own sense of usefulness (which, by the way, is not a good enough reason to lead from the front).

This is exactly the point that I was coming to realize in December: I realized that I, too, was a potential barrier, and that I needed to get out of the way, focusing on supporting, encouraging, and equipping people like Mario and Samuel to sell the strategy to their nation's own sons and daughters.

If something cannot be done when I am gone, it should not be done now. No cars, no computers, no certificates. No white guy, except as an encourager, equipper, and mentor. That will, I hope, facilitate the continuity of our program when I am gone.

If we can start out with as few barriers to sustainability as possible, the Mozambicans who continue the program after our departure will have few to dismantle or surmount.

Break the Rules!

So much for the rules. So much for our effort to avoid erecting barriers to the success of our program. Barely a week has passed, and already I broke the rules in a big, exciting way. Mario, Samuel, and I hopped aboard an airplane and flew to Nampula, a province in northern Mozambique, to witness a village-based savings and loan project being administered completely by Mozambicans.

Our desire in doing so was to demonstrate our commitment to the program by investing in Mario and Samuel as its coordinators, to create momentum to kick off their new jobs, and most importantly, to inspire them to see what Mozambicans can accomplish on their own. Through the trip, Glenn and I wanted to help them to cast a vision for themselves of what they could accomplish back home in Maputo.

And we had some fun along the way as well.

Nampula is Samuel's birthplace, but he left when he was five, in the midst of civil war, and has not been back since. He could understand a few words of Makua, the local tribal language, but not many. Mario had never been on an airplane before, though used to spend a lot of time at the airport with his father, before he passed away, watching flights coming in and going out.

Once in Nampula, we rented a four-by-four truck and quickly realized the wisdom of our decision. Many of the roads that we drove on were hazardous on the best of days, but we did not have the luxury of those "best" days. The sky poured rain every afternoon of our trip, and the roads became slippery, muddy paths carved out of the wilderness.

At one point, as we drove down a slippery incline, we squeezed our way past a bus stranded in the ditch to our left, and a pickup similarly ensconced to our right. The hole that we drove through was so tight that the driver of the unfortunate pickup had to roll down his window and fold in his side mirror for us to pass.

We were informed that there is no such thing as a street map for the city of Nampula, the capital city, so there was no hope of a map to guide us from one village to the next. "As long as you have a car, you have accommodation," were the wise words of one of my colleagues back in Maputo. He thought he was kidding at the time, and so did I, until we tried driving from the district of Ribaue back to Nampula, and somehow ended up in Mecuburi instead. I had noticed only one possible turn in our four-hour journey, and by the time we realized we were lost, that one turn was an hour or two in the muddy darkness behind us, so we pulled off the road into someone's field and camped for the night inside the crowded luxury of our truck.

(That night, I thought I stepped on a thorn—my foot stung as if I had stepped on something sharp. Weeks later, I learned that a jigger flea had taken up residence in the bottom of my foot, making a nest and laying a bunch of eggs. As the doctor cut a small hole in my foot and cleaned them out, he showed me pictures of the painful sores that often inflict barefooted children that come into his office with similar but much more severe infestations.)

We spent hours and hours in that rented truck, kept from weariness by the sight of dozens of people walking, from sunrise to sunset, along the same muddy paths pulling their loads by bicycle or atop their heads to the market like yoked oxen. Driving alongside their daily plight, our chore paled.

And, in one- or two-hour snippets of time between nearly 900 kilometres of mostly treacherous driving, we witnessed the value that village-based savings and loan programs are providing to tens of thousands of rural Africans.

We broke the rules in a big way this past week, and I hope that it was a valuable investment. On Monday morning, we will try to restore the discipline of no cars, no computers, no certificates. And no airplanes or rental trucks, either.

There Is Room at the Inn—but Nothing More!

In preparation for our trip to Nampula, I knew that we would have difficulty balancing my first-world expectations with Mario and Samuel's African standards. Any hotel that we selected, I thought, is likely to be below my standards and above theirs.

Despite some trepidation over the conditions that I would face, I wanted Samuel and Mario to be responsible for making decisions, including where we would stay. Our first night was spent in the small community of Ribaue. We stayed in the only accommodation that we could find, which cost us $4 each. My anxiety lightened as I heard the responses to questions that Mario and Samuel asked of the caretaker:

"Yes, the hotel has private washrooms," was the reply to their first question.

Of course, my anxiety was not in retreat for long. I soon learned that this is not the same as having a washroom in my room: what they really meant to say was, yes, our communal washrooms have doors on them. And I soon learned that those doors latched closed by the strength of a bent nail hammered into the door frame.

"Does the hotel have water?" Mario asked next.

"Yes," was the simple response, which (foolishly) was enough for me as well. The hotel has water! (Wait a second. Is it usual to ask if a hotel has water?) What I did not yet realize was that "having water" and "having running water" are two completely different standards, neither one of which I would even think to ask. Asking about the availability of potable water—now that is something I would think to ask in rural Africa, but of this there was little room for doubt. There was no potable water and there was no running water. The washrooms with the flimsy doors down the hall were equipped with a bucket filled with the cold water of an open, hand-dug well out back, qualifying its proprietors to indicate that, yes, they have water. That bucket of cold water was used for both flushing and bathing.

I was starting to get the picture that luxury this was not when having sheets on the bed was the next feature described to us. And that the mosquito net hanging above my bed would be a suitable deterrent, unless, of course, the mosquitoes were clever enough to find any of the dozen or so gaping tears in its side. (Mosquitoes in Mozambique, as it turns out, are rather clever and by morning I was rather bitten.)

Despite the shock of being plunged into rural Africa, I slept mighty well that night after a long day of travel.

The hotel we stayed at for the last two nights of our Nampula adventure was closer to my standards (though the fact that we had a room at all was enough after our night of the cramped, sweltering faux-luxury of our pickup truck). At $20 a night, it was a little steep for Mario and Samuel, but they had difficulty finding other options.

This hotel, they grinned majestically as they told me, had cable television and running water! Heated running water, we later learned, which made my colleagues feel like they had hit upon the big time. The only thing that it was missing was a reliable supply of electricity. We were in the comfort of heaven. What, after all, do we need lights for when we are trying to sleep?

Grassroots Banking

While in Nampula, Mario, Samuel, and I met up with ten groups of men and women, perhaps 200 people, who all expressed to us the benefit that has been brought to their lives through vil-lage-based savings and loan associations—the program that we want to import into the rural areas surrounding Maputo. These were 200 of the 27,000 people already involved in such groups throughout Mozambique, and over half a million around the world.

There is no need to reinvent the wheel when such a proven methodology can be borrowed and implemented in our own communities of influence.

We wanted to travel to Nampula to observe some of these groups first hand, to evaluate for ourselves whether or not they are having an impact on the lives of their members. And person after person, story after story, confirmed that the benefit is real.

The foundational component of the village-based savings and loan program is organizing community members into independent groups of 15 to 30 people for the purpose of saving money. The savings are not big: many people are able to put aside $0.20 each week, if anything at all; others have saved as much as $6 after a good week at the market, but that is rare. One group, with 22 members, saved a little under $4 this week: on average, $0.17 each.

Each group's members collect the savings and store them in a wooden box. Keys for the box's two locks are kept with two trustworthy group members, ensuring that the box is opened only in front of the group.

Some people question the security of the box. Could not it be stolen and opened easily enough with an axe or a rock? The group takes certain precautions, such as selecting a group member to store the box who has a secure house (which means having a front door that locks). The reality, though, is that assets are not secure in any place or any form in rural Africa. To underline that point, the leader of one of the groups we met with was absent: his goats had been stolen the night before, and he was off pursuing the thief.

We also asked about the necessity of the pooled savings concept. After all, could not each person keep their own savings in their own homes? Time and again, the women told us about the dangers of keeping money in their homes: before joining these groups, savings were always consumed by myriad little purchases at the market, or by neighbours who begged to borrow it, or by husbands who washed it down their throats at the local watering hole. The box, they said, injected discipline into their savings that was difficult to achieve on their own.

A second important element of the methodology is that group members can request loans from the accumulated capital, subject to approval from fellow group members. The terms are strict: often 30-day loans at 10 percent interest per month, but the group sets these terms themselves. Interest generated from loans is returned to the box to be distributed to deposit-holders at the end of the year. Because the group sets its own rates, and because no money leaves the group (as it does for commercial and microcredit banks), group members reported being satisfied with this lending option.

"We like being able to borrow from the box," one woman explained to me. "We no longer have any external dependencies."

Better still, because the group is on the hook for the loan if it is unrecoverable, the group frequently comes together to help a neighbour with a struggling business in order to improve the likelihood that the borrower will not default. This is personal banking at its finest.

Each group exists for cycles of one year at a time. At the end of the year, outstanding loans are repaid and savings are returned to deposit-holders with any interest accumulated from loans taken out over the year. Each member keeps a record of her savings so she can know precisely how much money she has stored in the box at any given time. Despite these records, the annual distribution always proves shocking. One woman knew that she would receive $40 at the end of last year, but was still in disbelief when distribution day came around. She had never held so much money at one time in her life. She described to us how she went home and carefully hid the money, and over the following days would open her hiding place, take out the $40 and just hold it in her hand and gaze at it before returning it to safety.

Members could put their accumulated savings back into the box at the beginning of the following cycle, but I did not meet anyone who had ever done that. Everybody has a place to invest their annual nest egg: school tuition for their children, a clay oven to start a bakery business, a field to grow vegetables, a bicycle to improve access to markets, pigs for reproduction.

One man, who lived under a leaky thatched roof, vowed that if he could ever save enough money to buy tin sheets to improve his house, he would sleep the first night on top of the new roof as a sign of thankfulness. When we spoke with him, he had recently completed his dreamed-about home improvements, and was nursing a cold that he caught sleeping in the rain on top of his house.

Story after story, people told us how their lives have improved as a result of being a part of these groups. That several of the groups were on their fourth yearly cycle is a testament that they believe there is real value in belonging to the group. Members of these well-established groups, who have been through several cycles of saving and investing, were most positive.

One young group explained to us that they had recently started after having seen the success of a neighbouring group. They had previously stayed on the sidelines as sceptics, until jealousy over the investments that the original group was able to make convinced them to form their own.

Of course, none of this means that the methodology is a panacea. Facilitating community members to mobilize into village-based savings and loan programs makes a valuable contribution towards fighting poverty, but is not a solution all by itself. It is not perfect, but we did not meet anyone who wanted to quit their involvement in their groups, either.

The Widow's Mite

I asked several groups to rank in the order of importance to them the three components of a typical village-based savings and loan program: savings, credit, and something called the "social fund." I was surprised to hear that, in each instance, the participants cited the social fund as being the single most important aspect of the program.

This was not intuitive for me: we had begun researching these types of groups as a way of eliminating some of the barriers to micro-enterprise development created by microcredit lenders and other organizations. I had thought that credit would be the most important, followed by savings (but even then, that savings only existed to provide sufficient capital for the credit program), and then the social fund a distant last. I had the order completely on its head.

The social fund (we might call it a benevolent fund) is not only a small self-insurance fund, but a way to build social cohesion within the group and community by allowing members to respond quickly to emergencies.

"The social fund is most important to us," one woman explained simply, "because through it we can help one another."

Here is how the fund works: every week when the group comes together to deposit savings, each member is required first to make a small deposit into the "social fund." The group decides how much is appropriate, but one metical per week (about $0.04) was typical. This social fund grows slowly, increasing by perhaps $1 a week.

If someone is not able to scrape together the required contribution, they could simply make a double contribution the following week.

Potholes, Padlocks and Poverty

The social fund adds a degree of complexity to the program that I was not sure was warranted by its meagre benefits. To be honest, I thought that the idea was a little silly. Meeting after meeting, the women and men who participated in these groups chipped away at my erroneous presumption. Had it not been for their overwhelming enthusiasm, I would have suggested scrapping the peripheral program as a needless distraction.

I dared ask a question that would never occur to me at home in Canada, but seemed obvious from my then-vantage point sitting on a caniço mat under a shelter built with mortar excreted from termites and a leaky thatch roof: is it difficult to save one metical per week?

The tone of the lady's voice who responded suggested that her answer was obvious: yes, of course it is. "But," she continued, "contributing to the social fund is a habit. I put aside enough money every week, just like I do for food."

The group collectively decides when to draw on the fund. All of the women I spoke with lit up when they recounted their ability to purchase medication for a neighbour's sick child, or to make simple funeral preparations for a deceased spouse, or respond to other unexpected events.

These families, living in rural southern Africa, are so poor that they could not otherwise afford a trip to a hospital room that would save the life of a child, even if that trip costs under $1.

These groups are community-based, not church-based, and many members are not Christians. Some are Muslim, others hold traditional beliefs. Regardless of their beliefs, the members of the group demonstrated over and over again what it would look like to have God's Kingdom realized here on Earth. Every week through these groups, God's Kingdom is made real in rural Africa by women and men who can scarcely afford to eat, yet can spare an extra mite to help a neighbour in need. Every one of them makes their deposit hoping that they can help a neighbour, but knowing that it could very well be their own family that requires emergency aid this week.

NOW, UNLOCK YOUR OWN MISSION FIELD

1. What is your definition of poverty? What makes someone poor? Why does this make them poor? Do they consider themselves to be poor as well? Are there any ways in which you feel poor?

2. Sweatshops have received a lot of attention in the media. Imagine that you were in charge of hiring somebody in Africa. How would you treat them? What would you pay them? As if they were in Africa, or as if they were in your country? How do your decisions positively and negatively impact their environment?

Challenge Yourself:

Like the widow who gave her mite, and like the women in Nampula who contribute $0.04 every week to the social fund even when it is difficult for them to do so, God wants us to have a generous spirit. Research a charitable organization in your area that can act as your social fund, select an amount, and give to them regularly. You never know when it will be your turn to draw on their assistance.

9 A Month Under Siege

Caught in the Middle

Mario and Samuel have just had their first encounter with the orange-eating group of oppositionist church leaders. That the leaders allowed them to come to the meeting at all was a small victory, considering that they have been rebuffing me since the fall. I will accept that as a tiny morsel of evidence that our nationals-first strategy of implementing this program is working: with Mario and Samuel in the lead, we were finally granted another hearing.

Of course, that we were granted another hearing is not to say that the leaders were completely ready to accept our ideas. The leaders provided our two new program coordinators with the same impassioned drubbing that they had given me.

Mario expressed afterwards that, despite our warnings, he was unprepared for their combativeness.

Samuel, who had been part of that very leadership team before accepting the current assignment, knew what he was up against but was still disheartened by their reaction. He understood the drive behind their bordering-on-belligerent behaviour, but now sees it as plain old selfishness.

They were, in a sense, caught between us, their employers, and them, their compatriots.

Mario and Samuel shared with the leaders the village-based savings and loan program that we learned about on our trip to Nampula. They explained that they see this program as a foundation that will serve to build up the financial capital necessary to successfully implement other programs: micro-enterprise training, chicken farm franchises, and more.

The unhappy leaders recycled their old complaints: they do not want to save their own money, and they do not want loans. They want us to give them money with as few strings attached as possible. Preferably none, please. But they would also like to participate in the first savings and loan association. I guess that is a sort of back-handed endorsement that they see merit in the idea, even if it is not their first choice.

Perhaps the best news of the day came afterwards, when Mario and Samuel expressed that they remain convinced that what they witnessed in Nampula would be positively received by communities here in Maputo and are determined to march forward. They have identified an ally among the group of leaders and are intent on implementing a pilot project in his community sometime in the first half of April. The clock is ticking....

The Trains Run On Africa Time

Back in January, Laura and I picked up a copy of Cape Town's official tourism visitor's guide. Its section labelled "local lingo" describes Africa time in the following enlightening way:

Just now: If a South African tells you that they will do something "just now," they mean they will do it in the near future but not immediately and possibly not ever!

In Africa, "just now" means "possibly not ever." Whenever I hear those words—just now—I can ignore the entire statement because it provides me no information at all. For example, what did

Simo, our host in Cape Town, mean when he said that he would get the keys just now for the garage door so we could lock up our little rental car? Did he mean now? Or sometime today? Or possibly never? As it turns out, he meant within half an hour, which surpassed my low expectations.

"Africa time" is such a widespread and well-practiced concept that, although the battery in my watch died six weeks ago, I have not been bothered enough to replace it yet. I guess I will replace it just now. (Of course, that is not to say that I have completely adopted Africa time yet. I still get stressed when we are running late—just ask Laura!)

Our empregada is here cleaning our house as I write and provides another great example of Africa time. She was supposed to come yesterday, like she comes every Wednesday. Without even a phone call she did not show up, and without a phone call she appeared at our doorstep this morning. Alzira explained to me that, by the time she realized yesterday that it was her day to come, it was mid-afternoon.

This has happened several times before: imagine our surprise the first week that she missed work, when a 7:00am doorbell interrupted our sleep the following Saturday. There stood Alzira, ready to clean. No problem, not for her, anyway. And no acknowledgment that it was anything other than Wednesday.

I am often sitting around wondering if she is going to show up just now.

I do not mean to leave an impression that Africans are lazy, or that they intentionally disregard time. Sometimes the deck is stacked against them. Sometimes the poor do not have the luxury of being on time.

I had a meeting scheduled recently with one such young man,

and he was decidedly late. Once the meeting had concluded, he apologized for his tardiness and proceeded to explain to me what had happened. He works for a restaurant, and his shift ended at 11:00pm the night before. He then usually takes a local minibus chapa home, but it was raining. Mozambicans do not like to work in the rain, and the privately operated minibuses are no exception. Once he realized that he was not going to succeed in getting a ride, he started the hour-and-a-half walk home, arriving home after 1:00am, soaked and exhausted. He overslept, but not enough to make him late for the meeting. What actually made him late was that he needed a clean shirt.

He only has two, or maybe three, shirts, so his choices are to wash frequently or wear them dirty. Africans, just like the rest of us, would rather not do the latter. The rain-soaked, dirty shirt from the day before needed to be cleaned.

But laundry is not a matter of throwing a shirt in the machine to gyrate on automatic while a quick breakfast muffin warms in the microwave. Not without electricity and running water. He first had to fetch water, and then had to wash his shirt by hand, hang it to dry, and hope that the sun is kind enough to dry it quickly.

And when all that was finally done, he had to walk over to the nearest paved street and hope that he was lucky enough to find a minibus that is running in the direction of our meeting (which it was) or start walking.

Good rules-of-thumb for working in Africa are to be sure not to schedule meetings after meetings—doing so rarely works—and have a little mercy for those who arrive late, too. Sometimes the trains are running on Africa time.

Feed My Sheep

Over the past number of weeks, many people have been asking

us about the impact of flooding in Mozambique. There has been a small amount of flooding in Maputo. Yesterday, Laura and I noticed a floor of water flowing through dozens of caniço homes in Alzira's neighbourhood. The major flooding—the emergency that has been broadcast on the international news—is occurring primarily around the Zambezi River in central Mozambique, perhaps 500 kilometres from our home.

David Morrison is a missionary colleague from Toronto, Canada, who is based in Malawi, bordering Mozambique to the northwest, where this major flooding has been occurring. He has been assisting with the relief effort by bringing trucks of maize meal and the Bread of Life to starving refugees, and he shares the following glimpse of his trip into Mozambique's newly established refugee camps last week:

> *It is 4 a.m. and we are barely awake as we load the last few relief items into what is already an overloaded Pinzgauer to begin our seven-hour journey back to Mozambique. Our convoy will bring hope and 17.5 metric tonnes of maize flour to some of the thousands who are suffering in the flood zone in Mutarara district. I am accompanied by three of our national church leaders: Timothy, Ali and Samson, who are squeezed in among beans, clothing, soap and salt, as well as supplies to sustain us on the journey, like clean water and 100 extra litres of petrol.*
>
> *The rains this week have made the roads more challenging. We drive slowly and stop to navigate our way through each washout before proceeding. The strength and manoeuvrability of the Pinzgauer get us through many difficult patches of flooded road. We see field after field of destroyed crops, collapsed houses, and several refugee camps with grass huts close together on isolated pieces of high ground. Our pas-*

tors in the back are bashed around as we make deep ruts in the muddy road. Mud shoots down the sides of the truck and splashes up on the windshield. After about 10 kilometres of driving, with heart beating fast, I am soaked in sweat from manoeuvring the truck through the challenging conditions.

We are carried by the strength of God, and His grace sees us through the borders and to our first destination—a refugee camp we visited the previous week. A place of great despair and suffering.

We pull off the road into the camp and are warmly greeted by the village headman and the other leaders. They are grateful that we have kept our promise to return, and look eagerly to see what we have brought. All are gathered and take refuge from the blazing sun under the shade of a large tree. Our church leaders begin singing praises to God.

The community is so welcoming. The people are so hungry. They tell us that already one person has died from hunger.

I start to cry—the situation before me is too over-whelming. Tears of sadness for the people's suffering mix with tears of joy knowing that on this day everyone will be filled. I hide behind my camera and start taking pictures. Moments later the truck in our convoy pulls up…and stops! The people's despair is quickly lifted from their faces. The songs of worship grow more passionate. Hope has arrived!

Until now the camp had been overlooked. For weeks its inhabitants have been hungry, eating grass, roots, bugs and lily bulbs from the crocodile infested flood areas. People are sick with malaria, dysentery, eye infections, skin infections and coughs. I see many babies with pus oozing from their eyes. Children have bloated stomachs and wear rags. Many of the young ones have nothing to wear at all.

I watch the village headman as the truck approaches. His face is filled with disbelief. Can this be true? Is this really happening? Is this food for us? For a moment he looks stunned, but moves quickly to make a plan to ensure that the supplies are distributed fairly.

Over the past weeks these people have stood in this very spot and watched as many trucks similarly loaded with relief supplies drive right past them on route to Mutarara. They have become used to being passed by. I share with them that Jesus knows their pain and He does not pass them by. I proclaim verses from Romans 8: "Who shall separate us from the love of Christ? Shall trouble or hardship, or persecution or famine or nakedness or danger or sword…or floods? No, for I am convinced that nothing will be able to separate us from the love of God."

People listen intently to the message and are wanting more.

The mood in the camp is changing. There is hope, peace and joy. Revival has come! Praise be to God!

The 287 families are called one by one to receive food. All is done with order and without any fighting. As well as 50 kilograms of maize flour, which should sustain a family for a month, each family receives a portion of beans, soap, salt and some clothing. The children who are naked receive theirs first. Those children in rags also take priority and receive new clothes. The patient wait for hope lasts several hours, after which we continue down the road to the next camp.

David Morrison lifted the spirits of these battle-weary refugees by reminding them that nothing—certainly not a flood—can separate them from the love of God. That same chapter of scripture, Romans 8, also includes the encouragement that *"we know that in all things God works for the good of those who love him"* (Romans 8:28). That may be hollow comfort for the people of Mutarara district right now, but its truth can be observed seven years after similar life-endangering flooding struck southern Mozambique.

The community of Khongolote has been a central point of our ministry here. It was there that Laura and I helped to lay bricks of a church building in 2004. It was also there that I held a micro-enterprise training course last fall. And it is there where Mario and Samuel will begin implementing the village-based savings and loan program.

That community would not have existed but for severe flooding seven years ago that washed away homes in other communities, forcing people to move to a previously unsettled patch of land. Africans are resilient people. They are survivors. The sun will come out, the floods will recede, and the seeds of new life will germinate and sprout up amongst the muck of this tragedy.

Don't Blink

Mozambique's flood waters are receding and the news cameras are shifting their focus to other crises elsewhere in the world. Blink.

As the water recedes, the full extent of the damage can be assessed. The government has estimated that cleaning up the mess will cost US$71 million, but that grossly underestimates the extent of the damage. More telling are the personal impact statistics: an estimated 494,000 people impacted, including 38 deaths.

Survival is assured only by the tenuous strength of a thread, as thousands depend upon the acts of selfless front-line volunteers like David Morrison and the countless people whose support allows them to fill their convoys of trucks with maize meal and supplies.

But for many in Mozambique, the real crisis is just beginning.

Over the coming months, hundreds of thousands of people will leave these temporary refugee camps and return to their homes to find little more than piles of mud. Their crops, which would have been harvested this month and stored to feed their families until the next harvest, have been washed away. There will be little to eat in the coming months, not to speak anything of excess to hawk at the market.

Those who do have excess to sell will have difficulty recovering their costs, having to compete against the tonnes of international food aid that will depress local market prices. The arrival of food is good news for the starving, but bad news for the small-scale merchants trying to make a living. The United Nations World Food Programme (WFP), which coordinates food aid in such crises, has said that they will purchase as much food locally as possible, and is asking donor nations for cash to do so.

The WFP's challenge is not restricted to feeding those families affected by the flooding. In the south of Mozambique, a short but intense heat wave this summer caused nearly three times as many hectares of crops to wilt as washed away in the floods. The heat wave did not make the international news because, well, watching video footage of a heat wave is like watching video footage of paint drying. It is dull. Raging floodwaters, low-flying helicopters, washed-out bridges and dramatic rescues all help the newscasters to compete against other shows that feed our Hollywood-induced attention deficits.

Despite the action-packed video footage, floods are slow-motion disasters. Judging by the date stamps on the emails that we received, Mozambique was flooding for at least six weeks before it was severe enough to make the news back home.

And its people will be recovering long after the last news crews sign their by-lines and file their stories.

Blink.

It is not realistic to think that the news could broadcast every emerging crisis around the world. That is not the point. But featuring these stories creates two opposing problems: first, that viewers assume that when there is not a story on the evening news, that there is not a problem. Far from the truth. Second, they paint these places as dens of permanent disaster, of places they would not like to visit.

Mozambicans that I have talked with are embarrassed that the floods make international headlines. They are embarrassed that the international community will think of Mozambique as a country that hobbles from one crisis to the next. They want the news to focus on Africa's humanity, not its poverty. They want people to know that many great things happen in Mozambique in all the space between the punctuations of tragedy.

When we turn the channel, they continue to live. When we send our aid cheques to the next country, they continue to live. When our attention shifts, they continue to live.

Don't blink.

Meet Alfredo

As is typical of many large cities, Maputo has a certain magnetism that attracts homeless people in search of the too-often-empty promise of a better future. Thousands of children, orphaned or abandoned, find that they are not exempt from this cruelty. Laura's friend Sarah, an American missionary living here with her husband and young family, shares the following story:

> Last night, on our way home from a local art fair, we were confronted by one of the many sobering realities of life here in Maputo. A young street boy approached us and asked for money, so we gave him $0.25 and suggested that he use it to buy himself some bread.
>
> Before long, he had returned and was asking for more money. We noticed that he had bought some chewing gum

from a street vendor. A little confused, but thinking perhaps that he was going to sell the gum for a small profit, we asked him why he had bought gum instead of bread.

We continued talking to this young boy. His name is Alfredo, and lives out here on the street. We asked him where his mom and dad were. "They are both dead." He has sisters in Panda, about seven hours north of Maputo, but no family here. His stepmother had brought him to the city but had later abandoned him.

This 11-year old boy, smaller than my son Kaleb, was hungry, desperate, dirty, smelly and wearing oversized, ripped clothes that exposed to the world his lack of underwear. After five minutes of listening to Alfredo's story, our kids piped up from the backseat, reminding us of our family verse: Matthew 25:31-46. Kaleb said, "Dad, I just keep hearing in my head, 'Whatever you have done to the least of these brothers of mine you have done it unto me.'"

We decided to do something unconventional. We took this boy home with us and gave him soap and shampoo so that he could take a shower. Kaleb, who is 9, picked out some new clothes for him. He would wear a Twins baseball jersey and shorts, white socks and some tennis shoes.

Fifteen minutes later, the difference in this boy was amazing. His dirty, sullen face was replaced with a bright, smiling one. His slacking posture was now more upright. The clean clothes and some soap and water washed away a bit of the depressing street life and shame that he is so accustomed to wearing. He and Kaleb played basketball in the front of the house, just like regular boys. No black. No white. No rich. No poor. Just kids smiling and having fun.

We decided to go out for a chicken dinner together. The restaurant we chose is a prime target for begging in Maputo, and chances are very good that our young Alfredo has been shooed away many times by the same staff that would now be serving him dinner. You should have seen this kid. He sat at the end of the table with wide eyes and watched closely what our kids did. He tentatively ordered a grape Fanta and chicken with French fries. He tried hard to use his fork and knife to eat, then gave in to the peer pressure and used his hands like everyone else. The kids all took turns writing their names and playing tic-tac-toe on scrap paper.

On our way to the restaurant, as we were sitting at a stoplight, an elderly woman came to our car window begging for money. Young Alfredo reached into his pocket and pulled out one of his coins that we had given him earlier. Reaching his hand out, he said, "Here, I have one. Let us give it to her." Can you even stand it?

Sarah and her family were touched by their encounter with this young boy, who could easily have remained anonymous and quickly forgotten. Instead, they have a new friend to watch for as they drive down the streets and to pray for with their children as they put them to bed.

The seed of an idea is germinating in their minds about starting a Saturday morning ministry for the abandoned and orphaned children of Maputo, taking them out of the city to land where they can run and play, where they would prepare food for them and let them shower and get clean clothes, and where they could be reassured that they are loved beyond measure.

Others have already made reality out of similar dreams. Mozambique has several homes for these malnourished, forgotten orphans. Not enough, perhaps, but homes nonetheless.

Our friend from Canada, Julie Collins, came to Mozambique for a couple of weeks this month to spend time loving some of these fortunate few who live in an orphanage in Zimpeto, just outside of Maputo. Julie loves to share story after story about the children she has met. She talks about their bracelets and other handicrafts, their toy cars with aluminium can wheels, and their car tire acrobatics. She tells stories of proud children who relish hearing their names spoken to them, many of them knowing their name as the only possession that is uniquely theirs.

Each of these children was, at one time, like Alfredo. And one day, Alfredo may be like one of these orphans who have found a home.

Kings of the Hill

Laura and I took a day off work to have Julie show us around the orphanage where she has been living and share with us what she has been experiencing in her weeks here.

In addition to housing some 350 orphaned children, the staff at the Iris Ministries centre in Zimpeto conduct several outreach programs, ministering to teenagers living on the street, ministering to patients in the depressing Central Hospital, and ministering to the people of all ages who—believe it or not—spend their days rummaging through burning and rotting piles of garbage at the city dump.

Laura and I rode with Julie, in typical Mozambique style, on the back of a flatbed truck to the dump. Once there, we encountered dozens of grown men, women, and children on the top of the acres of smelly, smoking mess. Many walked barefooted, seemingly oblivious to the shards of broken glass and sharp wires protruding out of the smouldering heap.

Some industrious people were making piles of metal to sell to a recycling plant on the edge of town. I am told that each worker has his or her own territory on the dump, his or her own corner of hell to sift through.

Potholes, Padlocks and Poverty

One man we stopped to talk to carried a small plastic bag. Scrap ends of bread collected from the dump were visible through the bag's translucent plastic.

I really do not understand how people can find things of value here. The garbage that is trucked onto the site comes from the dumpsters that have already been picked through while sitting on the city streets. These people find their daily bread by picking through whatever trash remains after what I had thought to be the poorest of the poor have taken their fill.

So prolific are the people making their living atop the garbage dump that a certain social infrastructure has sprung up to support them. Some enterprising individuals have set up a small market selling food and cold drinks as if it were the cafeteria of a standard workplace. One person operates a cellular-based pay telephone booth under a faded orange umbrella jabbed into the top of the heap.

Life on the garbage dump is decidedly normal for these people. They do not know anything outside of this harsh daily routine that leaves the children looking younger than their age and the wrinkle-scarred adults looking older than theirs.

The outreach program is intended to share the gospel and a small meal with those experiencing physical or spiritual hunger pangs. These people live spiritual lives, if not squarely Christian lives. Nobody would reject the offer of prayer, and nobody failed to show up for the offer of bread. One man had initially indicated that he could not come to the little hillside church for bread because he could not leave his things in the dump for others to steal. He later reappeared, his belongings stuffed into a small flower-patterned duffel bag that had surely been discarded by at least one previous owner.

Another person, a time-worn woman who had taken time out of her scavenging to speak with us, wanted to pray for us. More than half of the people who we spoke with professed that they attend a nearby church, pointing in directions just over this hill here or that one there.

Julie, who had come to Mozambique with a heart for children, was taken by some small boys at work on the dump. One of these boys was Fernando, who was spending his morning collecting a few items before heading off to school. Julie watched in amazement when Fernando saw the man carrying the translucent sack of bread scraps whom we had spoken to earlier: though just a small boy wandering a garbage dump, his heart was soft enough to pull a bun from inside his shirt and offer it to the hungry man.

Bruno, a small boy not befitting of his strong name, was less talkative. Where we met him on top of the dump, he barely opened his mouth except to gently squeeze out his name as if floating on a whisper. I asked him if he knew about the small caniço church at the bottom of the hill and invited him to return with us for some singing and some bread. I did not expect him to come.

I had mistaken Bruno's shyness for reluctance. He braved a smile when we saw each other in front of the church later that morning. I asked him if he had ever been to this church before. "Yes," he replied simply. He offered few other words. I told him that I had never been there before, which makes it his church and makes me his guest. He grabbed my hand and pulled me in the front door, and we sat together on a caniço mat laid out on the church's hard floor. He said only one other word to me the entire time. Pointing to the other side of the church, he said, "Julie." A friendly face that he had remembered from on top of the dump. Julie was over there, sitting with Fernando. Like Bruno, he had decided to come to church as well.

Laura sat in a third corner of the church, weighted down by what seemed like half a dozen young girls sitting or leaning on her lap. One of them wore Laura's sunglasses upside down on her face. All of them wore the smiles of children being loved.

Potholes, Padlocks and Poverty

Combating the rise of international child trafficking has forced the creation of rules that prevent the orphanage from taking children off the garbage dump and giving them decent shelter, food, and education, but God's compassion—and that of people like Julie who travel around the world to love forgotten children—mean that the children of the dump are valued as the children of God. That, after all, is their true identity, albeit too often hidden underneath the sooty garments of reality.

The Deafening Echoes of War

Flooding, drought, and cyclones have filled the news over the past month in Mozambique. The southern capital of Maputo has—for the most part—been spared these destructive forces.

Until now.

Laura and I sat at home, writing a few emails to friends and family, when the distant rumble of a strange African thunderstorm started. It must have been far off in the distance, because we could not see a cloud in the sky. The storm must be just over the trees.

The thunder claps rolled in with a fury, getting louder and louder. The shockwaves were more intense than I had ever experienced. At several points, I looked outside, believing that a truck had hit our building. We decided to shut our curtains in case the windows shattered. As I was standing in the front window doing so, I noticed one dark cloud off in the distance. Then I noticed that it had a tail trailing down to the ground.

The thunderous booms grew in power.

Neighbours' windows were blown out, but I did not realize that the experience was much more severe for others in the city until we made some phone calls. The country's largest armoury was on fire again, flinging old Soviet projectiles in every direction. For more than four hours, munitions as small as bullets and as large as vehicles were sent flying kilometres away, killing, maiming, and destroying houses.

I reached Mario by telephone. He told me that the armoury was in Malhazine, right beside Zimpeto. The same one that had exploded near the end of January. Suddenly the tragedy was brought a frightening step closer to reality for us: Julie and the orphanage are just down the road! Our cell phone reception was lost briefly as we tried to make contact. The electricity was spotty, as well. We finally received word back from the orphanage: please pray. Projectiles were flying over their heads. Everyone was huddled together in a small building, volunteers comforting orphans, volunteers comforting volunteers. It was a frightening, albeit accidental, war zone in an otherwise-peaceful country.

A shell tore through the roof of the chapel where the orphans were scheduled to be worshipping but thankfully were not.

Once again, by the grace of God, Laura and I were protected in our cocoon, but had no way of helping our friends as the danger unfolded.

I did not fully grasp the magnitude of what was happening until the next morning when I drove to Zimpeto to get Julie and bring her to the airport for her scheduled departure. Malhazine is right in between our home and Zimpeto, forcing me to drive by the now-quieted armoury. Crowds were gathered around trying to learn what they could. Holes were punched in large buildings; small, simple houses were flattened. Military personnel were gathering hundreds of unexploded 250 kilogram bombs from people's yards, placing them on the backs of trucks and parading them down the street to the false safety of their storage facility. Back to where the explosions started.

Once at the orphanage, the first person I encountered was a long-term volunteer whose children Laura teaches at school. She and her husband were visibly shaken, feeling the burden of caring for their own family and the hundreds of scared orphans under their watch. At that point, they still were not sure where all the children were: frightful of war, Mozambicans' habit is to run aimlessly.

The government is reporting the death toll at somewhere over 100. That is how many bodies are accounted for in the morgue, but everyone knows more will be found over the coming days. Hundreds of people crowd the hospitals maimed and wounded. The hospitals have run out of blood for transfusions.

I was relieved to hear that there were no injuries at the orphanage, and that Julie was fine, though shaken. We spent the morning at the airport, waiting for the uncertain hour of her departure as the airport's damaged runway was repaired.

By late morning, rumours were circulating that the explosions had resumed. Laura's school was closed early; Julie's orphanage was evacuated.

By early afternoon, the airplane that would take Julie home had arrived from Johannesburg, and the crew seemed more eager than normal to make a quick exit. As Julie boarded, I wondered if their haste was because the plane was so late already, or because of the black smoke visible on the horizon at the end of the runway.

Barely half an hour after landing, the plane had loaded its new passengers, refuelled, and was again airborne. It was soon a speck in the sky, distancing itself from the chaos below, safely on its way to Johannesburg.

A Lesson on Cellular Economics

It is Tuesday night. Laura has had a long day, and I am tired too. Come to think of it, it has been a long month. Neither of us particularly feels like making anything for supper, so we call Mimmo's. Tuesday night is two-for-one pizza night.

And an hour later we receive a lesson on cellular economics in Africa.

My cell phone rings, but only once. I retrieve it from the office, punch in the code to unlock it, and a message appears to tell me that I have one missed call. An unknown number.

At home, I would have just stopped there. Probably someone dialled the wrong number, realized it, and hung up. But that is not how cellular economics works in Africa. I suspected that this was the "Mozambican ring," so I hit redial. Sure enough, it was the pizza delivery man, lost. Five minutes later, we had our pizza, only slightly cold.

I wrote previously that cell phones are ubiquitous. That only tells half the story. Most people do not actually have any credit on their phones, so it is very common to receive a one-ring phone call. Call me back, please. On your credit.

In Mozambique, outbound calls are charged; inbound ones are not. That simple fact has a profound impact on cell phone usage here. Everyone with a cell phone is an amateur economist.

In Bangladesh, the Grameen Bank's "telephone ladies" made popular a micro-enterprise of what amounted to a roving phone booth: a lady would receive a loan for a cellular phone and make her living by selling airtime to people in the community who did not have telephone service but needed to make a phone call. In Mozambique, a similar model is used by South Africa's OneCell. Even in the capital of Maputo, the streets are splattered with OneCell's bright orange umbrellas, including the one that I saw on top of the garbage dump earlier this month. Under these umbrellas, entrepreneurs sell phone calls over a cellular network.

These, like the phone booth back home, will soon be extinct.

Everyone has a cell phone, but few have credit. Sounds like

prepaid credit is valuable, right? Right. In fact, it is a convenient way for people to store and transfer wealth. By punching in a particular series of digits, followed by a recipient's phone number, users can transfer credits from one to another.

Imagine wanting to purchase a small bunch of bananas from the sidewalk vendor, but not having any money left. Rather than handing him cash, you can instantly "deposit" some of your cellular credit from your phone to his (that is, if you have conserved your prepaid credits!).

For the vendor, having less cash means that there is less risk of being robbed.

And I hear—though I have not seen it yet—that there are even enterprising individuals who will purchase the street vendors' excess cell phone credit at a modest discount and resell it to people wanting to replenish their phones.

Cell phone credit, it turns out, functions as a second currency in Africa. Without, I would imagine, having to pay taxes to the government. Yet.

Now, Unlock Your Own Mission Field

1. Have you experienced someone not living up to your expectations? Perhaps they are always late for work, or perhaps they always cancel dinner plans, or perhaps they____(fill in the blank.) Take off your shoes and try theirs on for a few minutes. Write down reasons for which their circumstances might be contributing to their behaviour.

2. Read God's promises in Romans 8. Think about difficult situations in your past. From the perspective of hindsight, how has God taken this situation and turned it around for good? Do you trust that He has the power to do that again?

Challenge Yourself:

Who in your community is like Alfredo—the "least" of our brothers and sisters? What would it be like to give him or her a special evening—instead of crossing over to the other side of the street, try taking him or her out for dinner. Get to know this person's story: where he has been, where she hopes to go. And then remember this person in your prayers.

10 Starting To Step Back

The Smiles Are Free

A couple of months ago, I encountered a power struggle between two guards offering to watch my car. The $0.20 wage that car guards stand to earn causes a surge in these freelancing entrepreneurs, particularly at Christmastime. I agreed with the first boy who offered to watch my car, but quickly a second emerged. "Come on," he urged, "that is just a child. I am much stronger. I will watch your car."

I am just running into the vegetable market for a minute, I thought to myself. I proceeded to roll up a sleeve and flexed a rather thin arm, asking the older boy if he meant to imply that I did not have plenty of my own muscle. I told him that I already had a guard for my car, too. The young boy would do just fine.

Humour—if I can be so presumptive as to use that label to describe my little exhibition—seems to be a great diffuser of conflict in Africa. And a great way to gently point out that you cannot be taken advantage of by a vendor on the street.

"Come on," one market vendor whined in English when Laura and I expressed reluctance at the price he was offering for one of his products. "I sell these things for 350."

I looked him in the eye and smiled. And then I asked him in

167

Portuguese who actually buys those things for 350 meticais, aside from estrangeiros. Foreigners. I was not interested in the foreigner price, I told him.

His reply? "I will give it to you for 250."

We eventually settled on 220 meticais, which I think still yields him a handsome profit. Our rule of thumb is that the vendors' opening price—especially in tourist areas—tends to be about double what a good closing price should be. And the safety valve is that street vendors seem savvy enough to not sell their wares for a loss. They are not afraid to refuse a sale.

Street hawkers will use what little English they know in an attempt to woo tourists. The most common sound around the market is a voice calling from behind: "Best friend, best friend! I give you a good price!"

I could not resist joking with one of these vendors. "If we are best friends," I asked in my broken Portuguese, "why do you want to sell me these things? Why will not you give them to me as a gift?"

Another vendor quietly snickered and took a step back, realizing that I am not quite the easy target that I appeared to be.

"Ok, I will give you these things," the first vendor responded, not wanting to be outdone in the exchange, "but only if you will come next Saturday and help me to sell them!"

Neither of us thought the conversation was serious, which is what makes it most fun. We vigorously shook hands and included the cultural thumb-snap that only friends add and went in our own separate directions. He understood that he was not making a sale but had fun anyway.

"Best friend, best friend!" He was not gone for long. Give him credit for being tenacious. My mistake was glancing at a batik, which he was also eager to try to sell me. "Buy it so that you will remember Mozambique," he tried to persuade me.

"But I live right here in Maputo," I said. "What I am really looking for is a reminder of Canada. I will buy any souvenirs you have that are from Canada."

A laugh, a handshake and thumb-snap, and my best friend was off to make a sale to someone else. A real tourist.

Sitting on My Hands

My morning plans have been thwarted. I was planning on going with Samuel and Mario to a series of meetings with important people in Khongolote, where they will implement the first village-based savings and loan program. Mario and Samuel have been making their rounds, going from government office to government office, trying to get approvals here and permits there.

In Mozambique, it is a bad idea to begin any project without the knowledge and support of each community's government leaders. It is also difficult and time-consuming to secure that support. Samuel and Mario have been surprised by the amount of bureaucratic red tape, but the area administrators have been receiving them well. One administrator told them of some people who started "a development project" in their community a couple of months ago: in that case, the good Samaritan went from door to door collecting money ostensibly to start a loan portfolio, but pocketed the money and vanished. Past experience has proven that the government is right to be cautious and appears to like the features of our project that prevent the types of past abuses that the government officials have witnessed.

Back on the subject of these important meetings, it would have been good stroking for my ego to be able to go. Meeting with government leaders would have made me feel important, even valuable. I am, like many people, just insecure enough that I need to define myself by what I do. But yesterday, Mario suggested that he and Samuel should go to the meetings without me.

Some part of me—that little good angel sitting over my right shoulder—was quite pleased. I want them to risk being independent, to have the courage to work on their own. They will need to once I am gone, so it is great that they want to start now.

Just underneath Mario's bravery, he is timid. He is not entirely convinced that he is up to the job and would like Glenn or me to be there for support, to be there to answer difficult questions. But he also had the insight to recognize that the belligerent response that we have received from community and church leaders at past meetings is a function of our presence. He believes, because Westerners have come with pockets overflowing with money in the past, perpetuating the culture of dependency, that the community will not be happy with anything less than a handout this time as well—as long as I am sitting in the meeting as a symbol of that dependency.

"When they see Samuel and I," he said by contrast, "they do not see money, they see reality. They see that we [Mozambicans] need to work to get what we want."

For the sake of the program's success, Mario wanted to take a risk. To remove the safety net. Just as he will be forced to in two months from now, when Glenn and I have returned home.

I want the program to be successful too, but that little pointy-eared devil sitting over my left shoulder is busy pitching coal into the furnace, stoking the fire of my ego. If I am not there, nobody will know that it is my project. Nobody will understand the valuable contribution that I made, or give me the respect that I deserve. Nobody will....

But it is their project, not mine. I have been temporarily inserted into their story to light a fire, but it is their fire to maintain. It is their story. I will soon exit, and they will continue to live it.

The challenge with my empowerment approach is that making myself dispensable means that I am, well, dispensable. I am successful if I am not needed. The more successful Glenn and I are at mentoring and advising Mario and Samuel, the more I am forced to sit on my hands.

That is not an easy thing to do for those of us who find identity in hard work. But we must acknowledge that our Western results orientation is, at times, bordering on idolatrous. I am practicing idolatry when I act not in order to help, but to make myself feel important, or less guilty, or useful. In these situations, my work has become my god: that thing above which there is nothing else.

I could be sitting in another meeting, dragging it along, forcing my opinion, influencing the direction of thought. Making myself busy. In the great words of Paul, such people *are not busy; they are busybodies"* (2 Thessalonians 3:11).

So today I am sitting on my hands, not doing anything to advance this project. And if I want this project to outlive my stay in Mozambique, to build something truly lasting in only a year, sitting on my hands is exactly what I need to be doing.

Mario and Samuel will do a great job without me.

A Show-Off By Any Other Name

I recently had a discussion with a Mozambican brave enough to make himself vulnerable to me. And wise enough that I want to share his insight with you. At great risk to someone born into a relationships-based culture, he levelled the following criticism towards me and my kind: "Missionaries," he asserted, "are show-offs. Sometimes I think the only reason they come here is to show off."

Our conversation was interrupted, which gave me nearly 12 hours to think about what he meant. To reflect.

And then, the next day, I shared with him the substance of my reflection. "I think I know what you mean," I said. "We come here, we feel like we have given up a lot to do so, but here I am with a maid who cleans my house one day a week, a car in my driveway, imported foods on my shelves. This is all showing off, is it not? But," I added, slipping into a slightly defensive tone, "I do not think that missionaries come here in order to show off. I think they come here not realizing that they are showing off."

I was swiftly told that I had missed the mark. "We do not care about those sorts of things. Plenty of people here can afford them. Maybe 'show-off' was not the right word."

But the confidence to confront that he had wielded the night before was gone, leaving me again to search for the meaning of his words. This time, I found that meaning on my bookshelf, and it turns out that 'show-off' is appropriate, though in a more spiritual sense than I had been thinking. These are the reflections of Donald C. Posterski:

> Missiologists are now referring to "the coming of the third church." The first thousand years of church history were under the aegis of the Eastern Church, in the eastern half of the Roman Empire; the second millennium, the leading church was the Western Church. But in the third millennium the church will be led by the Third Church, the Southern Church–the church in the Two-Thirds World. Samuel Escobar reflects, "There is an element of mystery when the dynamism of mission does not come from above, from the expansive power of a superior civilization, but from below, from the little ones, those that do not have the abundance of material, financial, or technical resources, but are open to the prompting of the Spirit." [5]

Just because I come from the West does not mean that my relationship with these people in Africa can be unidirectional. We

---

[5] Posterski, *Enemies with Smiling Faces*, pp. 164-5.

often learn that giving is generous and that taking is selfish. That is true of material wealth, but the reverse is often true of things less tangible, such as knowledge and understanding: to be constantly the giver of knowledge and understanding is not only selfish, but also arrogant. There is nothing greedy about sitting down and trying to take—to listen and learn—a thing or two as well.

Bryant L. Myers, veteran of World Vision and professor of transformational development, expresses the idea that we Western missionaries need to work on developing bidirectional relationships in this way:

> *The non-poor, and sometimes development facilitators, suffer from the temptation to play god in the lives of the poor, and believe that what they have in terms of money, knowledge and position is the result of their own cleverness or the right of their group...[A]fter all, it is fun playing god in the lives of other people.*[6]

However "fun" it might be, I do not believe that missionaries in general suffer a deficit of good intention. Most make a huge personal sacrifice in an attempt to build the Kingdom of God. The trouble is, despite the silly advice given from a mother to protect the fragile ego of a child, it is not always the thought that counts. Intentions are hidden. They are invisible, and the result is that harmful acts, backed by good intentions, are still harmful acts.

This young African was trying to tell me that we Westerners have become spiritual show-offs, inflicted with a powerful dose of spiritual superiority. We have become the Pharisees of our day, off on a mission to point out everyone else's flaws, liberated to share our vast knowledge and understanding, but without realizing that Jesus beat us to Africa.

---

[6] Myers, *Walking with the Poor*, pp. 14-15, 115.

Some of my African colleagues have a far superior understanding of theology than I do. And they have a closer walk with Jesus than I do. They know that those who try to walk by themselves in Africa quickly stumble and fall. In the West, we have the crutch of consumerism to cushion our fall, so we often do not even notice when we are flailing in the dirt.

They do not always agree with me on the finer points of theology, but did not the apostle Paul accuse the wealthy people of the church of Corinth that their understanding was "but a poor reflection as in a mirror"? That the reflection is poor is important, yes, but equally so that it is a reflection. Reflections are backwards. Those words always sting me back to humility whenever I think that I have been bitten by a bout of spiritual superiority.

Tired

A sun is setting on a common criminal.
The gathered crowd forces an old car tire around his neck.
A spark is lit, then a blazing fire.
Hearts pound to the rhythm of drips of flaming rubber hitting the ground below.
Screams of pain echo past the crowd's silent relief.
Justice and injustice are fused together in this most awful crucible.
Where guilt ends and innocence begins, no one is quite sure anymore.

This tragic scene could be ripped from the US Civil Rights era or from South Africa's struggle to loosen the noose of apartheid.

Lessons have been passed on from one oppression-weary generation to another.

But this scene comes from present-day Mozambique, brought

STARTING TO STEP BACK

about by desperate neighbours frustrated by the height of crime. And frustrated by the inaction—or outright complicity—of the justice system. Police officers are accused of being paid off by criminals in exchange for front-door prison breaks.

Mozambique is tired.

"Give me your cell phone."

As Samuel told me of his experience at the Xipamanine market this morning, he recounted being slow to understand the boy's request. I like my cell phone, he thought to himself. I want it.

"I want to keep my cell phone," he responded naively to the boy's repeated request.

"You do not understand," the boy said. And very quickly, Samuel did understand.

Very quickly, there were six boys where the first had stood alone. Samuel was surrounded, then on the ground. A fist struck his jaw, and a knife cut somewhere through the confusion.

As Samuel recounted the story, he still wore a shirt with two slashes in the back and one on the left shoulder. A plastic bag held more destroyed clothing, but luckily the knife did not penetrate deep. Samuel's skin will heal.

His fear welled up; so did his eyes. He cried for his clothing, for his cell phone. And he cried for his country. "Mozambique," he said to me, shaking his head, braving a smile.

Samuel is tired.

His cell phone has been taken. It will cost a month's salary to replace, unless he goes to the black market to buy a stolen one. Those are the choices he faces: losing a month's salary, or rewarding the crime of his attackers.

A rich benefactor buys him a new cell phone to dull the pain of the loss. I do not mind. The cell phone may be a month's salary for him, but for me it is just a fraction of what I keep hidden in my sock drawer.

Xipamanine market is crowded with people, but nobody sees Samuel's attackers. Not a person helps. Not a person notices.

Today, the thieves slip safely into anonymity. If they attack another, they may not be so lucky. Eventually, the community will rise up with matches and an old car tire. A series of petty thefts will turn into the irony called vigilante justice.

Mozambique is tired.

Slaying Apathy

We cannot help but stare need in the face. And I must admit that sometimes it is tiring. It is tiring looking like the rich man in a poor country. Tiring being the rich man in a poor country.

And sometimes that fatigue crosses the line into the deadly territory of apathy.

I briefly stumbled across that line yesterday.

A young man stopped me on the side of the road and asked for some food. "I do not need money," he said, "I am hungry. I have AIDS, and I take free anti-retrovirals from Doctors Without Borders, but I do not have food."

He pulled out a card that documents his illness, but the proof was in his sunken, hollowed out face. He was definitely ill.

And yet that little fraud-busting voice whispered a protest in my head. The one that is well attuned to scams in Canada. The one that has decided that every story I hear on the street is spun in an effort to rip me off.

I nearly walked away. I even told him that I did not have anything for him.

I could have walked away. I could have gone home, emptied

my pockets of my coins and stacked them on my bedroom dresser where they would sit unused. I could have spent an extra ten minutes sitting at my computer working on well-intentioned micro-enterprise something-or-other, theorizing about how I could improve the lives of those unfortunate people around me.

Or, just as likely, I could have used the time to read one more article in today's newspaper.

But then who would have helped him?

Fortunately for that young man, my apathy was washed away by a shower of better judgment. How can you sit comfortably in your office and make plans for rescuing these people if you will not even look this man in the eye and offer him the assistance he is requesting?

That was the voice of God. I could nearly feel His hand reaching down from the heavens and grabbing me by the shirt collar.

It is not like I do not do anything, I protested. Is not that why I am here? Earlier this week I even bought a bushel of bananas just to leave beside the garbage dumpster so that the scavengers would have a decent meal. I am doing good work, right?

I did not need to ask this man what consolation it would be to him that I had helped someone else another day. He needed my help right then, and I was able to provide it. Perhaps I had to modify my schedule a little, and perhaps there would even be a moment or two of discomfort, but it was my turn to help.

Ok, I will help, I conceded to my better judgment.

We walked together to a supermarket to purchase some food staples. Inside, the ghost of a man gathered enough strength to pick up a large bag of rice. The kind that is made of burlap so that it does not split open and spill its contents all over the aisle of the store. Large enough to feed him for a month, he told me.

We agreed on a smaller bag of rice, and added a bag of beans, and a bottle of cooking oil. If the large bag of rice would have fed him for a month, our new purchases should feed him for a week, but I think that exaggerates the quantity of my help. He would make it last a week, is more likely.

Something rose up within me today to slay the apathy that I felt. It is not being too dramatic to suggest that had it not been defeated, my apathy could very possibly have slain this young man.

And I would have had an extra $4 on my dresser, and an additional ten minutes to put my feet up in the comfort of my padlocked apartment.

A Motley Crew

Time—the precise time, anyway—may not be important in Africa, but that is not to say that no matter is urgent. That little lesson was reinforced as I sat at a local church meeting with Mario and Samuel about some project details.

I had been expecting a call from our landlord for the past several weeks, ever since he asked Laura if he could take some of the bars off of our windows to re-use them in another apartment. They are redundant, so I did not mind, though I am not sure in Mozambique whether or not I would have legal ground to argue even if I did mind.

Weeks later, this is the day that he finally called. "The workers are here now," he said, "Could you be home in ten minutes to let them in?"

I have waited for this call for weeks, and now you want me home in ten minutes?

I was planning on returning to work out of my home office soon. "Give me 40 minutes," I replied. That gave me enough time to quickly wrap up the work I was in the middle of at the church and get home.

When I arrived at home, I was greeted by the crew that the landlord had hired to remove the bars. Three young men, none of them yet 20, all wearing tattered street clothes. One held an old and well-used screwdriver, another a hammer, and the third a standard kitchen knife.

Under any other circumstances, I would have been afraid.

Once inside, they asked me for a screwdriver that would actually fit into the heads of the screws they were trying to remove.

Remember, labour is cheap. The proper tools are not. I did not have a proper screwdriver either.

They hammered and chiselled away at the stubborn screws. Several times, I was sure they were going to slip and shatter the window. The thought had occurred to them as well. They debated amongst themselves leaving the most difficult of the three sets of bars, and forfeiting the $2 prize that they stood to split between them once they had successfully completed their mission.

Doubts aside, they persevered. Eventually.

"It will just take 20 minutes," the landlord had assured me over the telephone, "and then you can be back on your way." It was at the hour-and-40-minute mark that I looked up to see that the motley crew had woven my clothesline through the bars and were yanking furiously to try to free them from the window opening.

That was just 20 minutes after I had looked up to the sight of the boy who appeared to be the foreman standing precariously, partly propped into the air by a windowsill and partly by the shoulder of his crew member. I got a ladder from the other room, and they thanked me.

When the crew was finished their assignment, they promptly left. Their work may have been urgent, but those three panels of iron bars are still sitting in my home, though no longer affixed to the window. I do not know when the landlord will come to pick them up.

He will probably need them urgently next month, when I have long since forgotten that they are sitting there. And no doubt my phone will ring when I am doing something somewhere else.

Blessed Are the Poor

I have for months had a question tucked away in my back pocket, waiting for the right opportunity to pull it out. Asking it bore an element of risk, I thought, because it might convey a lack of understanding or sensitivity. After all, is not the answer obvious?

We are starting to take steps out of this world already, so I need to ask questions now if ever I am going to fully understand. I took the opportunity to pull the question out and lay it on someone who makes less in a month than I have ever made in a day since graduating from university: do you consider yourself to be poor?

"No, I am not poor. Of course, I am not rich either. To be rich would be to not have to worry about where my next meal was going to come from."

Never having had to worry about where my next meal was going to come from, I realized that poverty is definitely relative. Who in Canada, having made less than $1,000 in the previous year as the head of a household, would not consider him or herself to be poor? As he continued speaking, I became more and more intrigued by his reflections.

"I was rich once, you know."

He went on to describe for me that he used to live as the personal assistant for a wealthy foreigner here in Maputo. He earned a salary of slightly under $150 per month, but was also given accommodation and access to his patron's refrigerator. He had a life free of worry. A life of wealth.

"And being rich," he had come to realize, "is boring."

"I remember once when I did not cook for an entire week," he explained to me. "I just ate these soups that my patron had in the

180

cupboard, the kind where I just had to pour in boiling water, and had ham sandwiches grilled in a sandwich maker."

(I thought quietly to myself at that moment about all the times that Laura and I have picked up the telephone and ordered in food because we were just too tired or could not be bothered to cook something as simple as a grilled sandwich.)

"But I was often lonely, just looking after his house while he was away on business."

For this one Mozambican, life's objective is not riches. It is being in positive, meaningful relationship with neighbours. It is being able to live up to his God-given potential, which, he learned, is not sitting around babysitting a house that sheltered him from worry. A little bit of worry, he seemed to be suggesting, is the adventure that adds spice to life. The spice that keeps us relying on God rather than ourselves.

And in that moment I was more sure of this one fact than I have ever been in my life: that the objective of my international compassion ministry should be to equip people so that they are able to live up to their God-given potential, not simply to provide food for the hungry.

The poor are not those who cannot afford a Jaguar, or even a jalopy. The poor are those, with or without their jalopy, who are barred from realizing the potential that God has created within them.

Step Up, Mollywood

I know that you have heard of Hollywood. Everyone has heard of Hollywood.

And if you are a real film aficionado, you may even have heard of Bollywood, India's burgeoning answer to Hollywood.

Now, let me introduce you to the new kid on the block, which I will dub Mollywood. Hollywood Mozambique—one of the

many positive things that are happening in Mozambique.
Probably the first movies that come to mind are *Blood Diamond*
(2006, Leonardo DiCaprio) and previously, *Ali* (2001, Will
Smith), but those are not Mollywood. They are just the product
of Hollywood looking for inexpensive and authentic-looking sets
in Maputo.

This afternoon, Mario took me to the Theatro Gil Vicente on
Avenida Samora Machel in search of the real Mollywood, to catch
the matinee viewing of "O Jardim do outro Homem" (Another
Man's Garden). Yes, Mollywood, though smaller than most movie-
producing meccas, exists. Mollywood even writes, directs, and pro-
duces its own films. For this 80-minutes-plus-intermission,
Mollywood was thriving.

No matter that the theatre, a cavernous and aging Portuguese
monstrosity designed for stage plays not shown in decades, had all
of six people in it. Perhaps the price was a deterrent, though at
about $1.50 per ticket for the Monday matinee, I would have
imagined that a few more people would have bitten. Maybe the
after-dinner crowd is bigger, but I doubt big enough to fill the theatre's 1000 or more seats.

The film that Mollywood projected on the screen was categor-
ically not Hollywood. There were no explosions, despite this
country's infamy with landmines. And I could have seen more guns
standing on the theatre's steps looking out towards the street than
I saw captured on film (the latter featured a grand total of zero).

Instead, the film showed a culturally accurate portrayal of the
obstacles that a teenaged Mozambican girl faces in her quest to
qualify for university and become a medical doctor. The film
addresses many of this country's biggest issues: HIV/AIDS, corruption and coercion, petty theft, and poverty.

Its title, reflecting persisting gender discrimination, is a deriva-
tive of the traditional sentiment in Mozambique that, "sending a

girl to school is like watering another man's garden." A complete waste of time. Paying to educate a daughter is useless because her lot in life will be restricted to raising and feeding the children of someone else's son.

At several moments in the film, I shifted uncomfortably in my seat. After one of the plot's critical moments, showing a male teacher advancing on a student in exchange for the promise of better grades, I thought of Captain Jack Sparrow. "This is as real as *Pirates of the Caribbean*," I asked with my eyes, not uttering a word. It is just a movie, right?

"It is very real," Mario assured me, understanding my silent discomfort. Mollywood punches with the strength of reality, producing socially charged and relevant cinema that would be dismissed as drab documentary by Hollywood's red-carpet crowd.

Mario felt encouraged by the film's message of strength in the face of adversity. I was not encouraged so much as speechless and contemplative. Sometimes reality is hard to swallow.

Now, Unlock Your Own Mission Field

1. What might it mean to have a "god-complex"? Is there any area in your life in which this might be true?
2. How would you respond if you witnessed violence around you? How would you respond if someone came to you in need? How would Jesus have you respond, using the gifts, abilities, and character that God designed uniquely in your being?

Challenge Yourself:

Rent a film that wrestles with an issue of foreign culture: Hollywood films such as *Blood Diamond* or *Hotel Rwanda* would be fine, but foreign-made films would be better, if you can find them in your local video store. Invite some friends, and invite some members of the film's subject culture. Pop some popcorn. Insert yourselves into the movie. Discuss the movie as a group.

11 Reflecting (With a Broken Mirror)

Seeds Begin to Sprout

On Sunday, Laura and I packed into a Land Cruiser and headed for a church in Intaca, a small rural community about an hour outside of Maputo. The entire excursion was about six hours long, much of which was driving along abusive muddy roads and narrow, thornbush-lined footpaths. It would have taken less time had we known exactly where to go, but with roads that do not have names, in a village that does not have maps, in a community spotted with caniço home after caniço home, everything looks the same. And all roads seemed to lead to one particular building with peeling white paint.

From that intersection, we tried every possible direction. Straight, left, right—every attempt led back to that familiar peeling white paint. Frustration mounted as everybody in the car had different advice on where to turn next. It did not take long to realize that everybody was long on opinions but short on knowledge.

Once we had finally extricated ourselves from the quagmire of muddy paths, we found Intaca church. We were very late, but church had not yet started. In fact, nobody seemed to know what time it was supposed to start; people start walking from their homes when they hear that singing has started. And late as we were,

185

nobody was in a rush to get the service started. When we arrived, Olga, the pastor's wife, gave us a tour of a sewing training centre that she and her husband operate.

Laura and I wanted to visit Intaca because Olga and her husband Ricardo are looking for ways to partner with Semente Para A Comunidade—the Portuguese name that Mario and Samuel have given to our economic development program—to increase the number of sewing machines that they have in order to meet demand for their training program. These sewing machines are the old-fashioned pedal kind that do not require electricity. The women use them to learn to make school uniforms for their children and decorative linens to sell in local markets. But they are also prohibitively expensive for these poor rural women.

Mario and Samuel hitched a ride with us part way. They were headed to the church in Khongolote to invite congregants to an inaugural village-based savings and loan program meeting next Saturday. Because they asked, I decided that we could again break the rules and give them a ride, saving them a two- or three-hour minibus ride. But I did not want to be at the church for the meeting: it is their program. Afterwards, Mario and Samuel reported significant interest from the church.

Another opportunity for the Semente Para A Comunidade program (which literally means Seed for the Community, reflecting the potential for economic growth) started taking root when Samuel recently met with a local bakery run by a Christian woman. She is tired of employees who cheat and steal and whose drinking the night before makes their morning work less than productive. She is looking for opportunities to partner with Semente to provide employment opportunities to church members. Samuel and Mario, through the Semente program, would be responsible for identifying potential employees and providing them with Biblically based moral-standards training.

These ideas are slightly divergent from what I had originally envisioned for the program, but that does not make them bad. They provide an avenue for the church to be a good witness to the community; they also conform with the program's vision of removing barriers to economic development for church members. These are the exciting ideas that spring up when Mozambicans are empowered to have control over their own program rather than merely being implementing agents of a foreign-concocted scheme.

A Fractured Understanding

As I am writing—May 2, 2007—Canadian philosopher Charles Taylor is being awarded the $1.5 million Templeton Prize for his lifetime's work of arguing that problems such as violence and racism can only be solved by considering both their secular and spiritual dimensions.

This award will come as a surprise to many who draw a sharp line between the secular and spiritual realms. Many Christians in the West compartmentalize our lives in this way, limiting prayer to spiritual problems and our own intelligence and hard work to solving "real" problems. Atheists dismiss prayer as a psychological exercise at best.

"We will pay a high price," Taylor says, "if we continue to allow this muddled thinking to prevail."

Taylor's work would be received by most Africans as being, well, obvious. He might as well have won a boatload of cash for arguing that the sun is hot or that the rain comes from clouds.

Africans readily accept the role of spiritual influences and causes underlying physical events. Many access traditional spirits for protection, divination, and healing from witchcraft. Several people have impressed upon us that these practices are "very, very common," and every time I am struck by the emphasis that they use. A Mozambican woman with whom Laura works was bold enough to say that easily 95 percent of people still practice traditional beliefs. "If they say they do not, they are probably just hiding it."

Mario's mother recently asked to borrow money from him to buy a goat to bring to a sangoma. Being a Christian and knowing that God forbids witchcraft and divination, he would not lend it to her, but faces pressure to abide. Sangomas often ask for goats or chickens. They use the heads and feet to make healing potions and keep the good meat for themselves. It is a good deal for the witch doctor, Mario thought. They are well-fed.

Africans who engage the services of such traditional spiritualists are often looking to detect and cure physical or spiritual ailments, looking to foretell or alter the future. Perhaps they want to identify and punish someone who has committed a crime against them.

The practice is pervasive, though often hidden beneath society's veneer. I have heard stories of Christian ministers consulting these practitioners in an attempt to secure leadership positions within their churches. I have heard similar stories of government leaders.

This inclination towards seeing the world in its unfractured reality leads African Christians to be very spiritual people, and leads Africans of many faith practices to be keenly interested in discussions of gods and spiritual powers—often more so than the Western missionaries who have come wanting to teach them.

Some African traditional practices, like divination and witchcraft, are clearly inconsistent with Christianity, just as those of us in the West who rely on rugged individualism rather than on God are similarly inconsistent. That notwithstanding, African Christians struggle to see why some Western missionaries preach that reliance on God is incompatible with healing using the natural restorative properties of tree roots and bark, while these same missionaries can themselves pop a Tylenol Gelcap to soothe their own aches and pains. Africans wonder whether Westerners dance dangerously close to an idolatrous devotion to science, while Westerners believe that tradition-adhering Africans are themselves tapping their toes clearly in the polytheistic danger zone.

Each group, focused on the faults of the other, believes that its own practices are safely within the acceptable bounds of Christianity.

Charles Taylor is onto something. But it is not enough to look at the world through our own physical and spiritual lens: we must try to look through our neighbour's as well. Even those of us, like Charles Taylor, who acknowledge an integrated spiritual-physical world, lack the wisdom of God. Now we see but a poor reflection as in a mirror.

A Corrupt Chicken and a Broken Egg

Corruption is a risk wherever there are people vying for positions of power; that is to say, it is a problem in every corner of this Earth.

According to Transparency International, a watchdog dedicated to reporting on corrupt practices, 99 countries do a better job of fighting corruption than does Mozambique. That is not great. It is not even good. But it is not surprising given that the organization argues that there is a strong correlation between poverty and corruption.

There is a positive spin to the story: if corruption and poverty are positively correlated, then Mozambique is less corrupt than its poverty ranking implies it ought to be. By comparison, the UN's Human Development Index ranks 168 countries ahead of Mozambique.

Many people assume that if poverty and corruption are positively correlated, then one must cause the other: that corruption causes poverty or perhaps poverty causes corruption.

Potholes, Padlocks and Poverty

There are consequences to either interpretation.

To suggest that corruption causes poverty implies a moral flaw in the people of poor countries. They are inherently corrupt, and because of it they suffer poverty. This is dangerously close to arguing that the poor deserve to be poor, that their poverty is their own doing.

The converse is that people in poverty feel that they have little choice but to be corrupt in order to feed themselves and their families. But this interpretation allows people to shirk responsibility for their corrupt acts. We will stop being corrupt when we stop being poor.

The government of Mozambique opposes this latter interpretation, but to others it is compelling. Not that people ought to have their corrupt acts excused because of their poverty, but that the institutions of civil society that serve to uncover corruption require some degree of social infrastructure more readily available in wealthy countries in order to be effective guardians of society. A base level of education for all citizens, for example, would empower the citizenry to realize the social and economic harm that corruption causes and stand up against it.

The stereotypical image of corruption involves a government bureaucrat accepting a briefcase full of cash in exchange for some favourable act. And sometimes this is true. Mozambique has certainly experienced some lavish examples of alleged corruption and cover-up, some even involving the president's own family.

In reality, a lot of bribery is more subtle. It can even sneak up on the unwitting participant, and it is not always easy to stand up against.

I was recently riding in a car with a colleague when he was pulled over by a police officer standing on the road's shoulder. After having been detained at the side of the road for 30 minutes, it was becoming increasingly clear that the police officer would not let us go without paying her 500 meticais ($20) on the spot. When my colleague rightfully protested, asking instead for her to write a ticket that he could later pay at the police station, the officer delayed further.

He eventually capitulated and paid the officer the 500 meticais that she demanded, which almost certainly constituted a bribe. We cannot be sure she pocketed the money, but the scenario clearly fails the sniff-test of petty corruption.

I felt badly for hours afterwards, not because the driver had complied with the demands of the officer, but because we had done so in the presence of Mario. We modeled complacency—even acceptance—of corruption in a country trying to fight itself free of the grip of this scourge.

The next day, Mario expressed feeling guilty for having participated in a corrupt act.

Ultimately, it does not matter whether poverty necessitates corruption or corruption leads to poverty. In reality, both are probably causally linked to some broader complex system.

Whatever the cause, poverty and corruption are inextricably linked. If more people were like Mario, a poor Mozambican with a heart to improve his country, Mozambique would quickly rise up the ranks of Transparency International's scale and rid itself of corruption.

A Differential Diagnosis

Six years ago, I stood amongst real, as-seen-on-tv poverty for the first time. I was on a two-week study trip to Managua, Nicaragua. I remember clearly standing in our single-storey hotel, or perhaps it was a compound. The man guarding the door advertised his power with a larger gun than I had seen outside of Rambo movies my entire life.

I remember brushing my teeth and, out of habit, wetting my

toothbrush using the strictly forbidden tap water. And I remember the terror of not knowing what was going to happen to me for having committed a breach of this magnitude. Perhaps there is a room in the basement of the hotel packed tightly with the remains of those who had committed the same grievous sin. Or perhaps the ill effects on my health would be a slow and painful reminder for the duration of my life.

This is a different world, I thought. An uncomfortable world.

While in Nicaragua, I learned things about this world and our world—the two are, after all, inseparably knit together, arguably a single world—that were so shocking that they would take several years to soak into my being.

What I remember most about the trip was a conversation with our facilitator, Pastor Jon, about what appropriate responses to poverty ought to be. We were talking about all sorts of things that we had witnessed over the previous dozen days: about the benefits and risks of wealthy countries like Canada practicing "tied aid," about the harmfulness of improving people's housing by forced relocations, about self-empowerment through fair trade and cooperatives. Our interpretations of the previous days did not always agree. He seemed to be casting thunderclouds over the best efforts of the Western world to reduce global poverty. In our arguments, I took the pragmatic road and he the idealistic. Me the rational and he the fanciful. And I distinctly remember the apex of the conversation, when the wisdom of all of my 22 years focused down to a sharp, irrefutable point.

I had him right in my sights, and I pounced with what I was sure would be the decisive, knock-out blow in our debate: "You are telling me that you do not want to help these poor people realize economic improvement?"

How can you stand in the midst of all of this poverty—all of these starving children with threads of clothing hanging off their stick-thin bodies—and reject economic development as a solution?

"That is exactly what I am saying," he calmly replied. And with that, he wriggled out of my trap.

Fast forward six years into the future (I have become wise enough to know that I do not have all the answers anymore), and I am again standing amongst a similar degree of poverty, albeit in a different tucked-away, nearly forgotten corner of the world. Only now am I beginning to understand what Pastor Jon was trying to say.

He was, perhaps, trying to be a little provocative. No, he did not want those children to waste further into the gutters of history. Instead, he was opening my eyes to an interpretation of poverty that goes beyond a lack of stuff.

With his comments percolating in my mind over these past six years, I am finally prepared to agree with his wisdom. Poverty is not always about a lack of stuff; Pastor Jon would argue that it is never about a lack of stuff.

The solution that we find to poverty will necessarily be determined by our own interpretations of its causes. In his book, *Walking with the Poor*, Bryant Myers proposes some cause-response pairs as examples:

> *If the poor lack things, the response is relief and social welfare.*
> *If the poor lack knowledge, the response is education.*
> *If the culture of the poor is flawed, then they must become like us.*
> *If the social system makes them poor, then the system ought to be changed.*
> *If the poor are sinners, then they need to be evangelized.*
> *If the poor are sinned against, then we need to work for justice.*

But even our worldview interprets for us our reading of these cause-response pairs. There is something more fundamental underlying each of these pairings: does the locus of control for reshaping this world lay with us or with them? Does it flow necessarily from my desire to empower the poor that I am suggesting that I have power that they lack and can pass it on to them? Perhaps so; perhaps that is the truth. Or perhaps not.

The responses that we so often bring to the developing world reflect our god-complexes: that we hold the key—the power—to progress, and once we deliver this key to the developing world, they will become more like us. More forward-looking. They will improve.

These god-complexes suggest that we have all of the answers, and the developing world need only sit and listen attentively, take good notes, and all will be fine.

Even the labels that we choose to apply connote this interpretation: the developing world is behind us, but they are developing. Soon they will catch up and be just like us. The First World is, after all, Number One.

What is required is a *differential diagnosis*. That is a label that doctors use in complex medical situations (as popularized by the maverick television doctor, Gregory House) and which Jeffrey Sachs has borrowed for international development. The complex label makes this simple statement: there is no single cure for poverty.

People experience poverty in different ways.

People are poor for different reasons.

A one-dimensional understanding of poverty will, by necessity, be an incomplete understanding.

Calamity's New Face

A journalist reporting in the midst of Mozambique's brutal civil war once wrote about a young girl who, standing near him, pointed to the sky and whispered, "calamidades." Calamity. The year was 1988, and the journalist was in Morrumbala in the province of Zambezia. By the journalist's account, he did not know what to expect. Perhaps the keen young observer was tuned into the early rumble of an incoming war plane or perhaps warning of the onset of a torrential downpour that could lead to an equally devastating flood.

The journalist looked to the sky, to the southeast where the girl's small finger pointed, and saw nothing.

The rain fell gently. The child, thin, shivering, and clad in burlap, continued to point to the sky, repeating the word: calamidades.

Calamidades was the child's shorthand for the Mozambique government's Department for the Prevention and Combat of Natural Calamities, and what this particular child noticed was a distant airplane approaching the airstrip near the Morrumbala mountain. The calamity, as it turned out, was already present in her starving body, and her ears were acutely tuned to the hum of relief approaching from a distance.[7]

Nearly 20 years have passed since that plane arrived in northern Mozambique, bringing food and clothing to that weary child and her family. In June 1999, with civil war comfortably behind the country, the corrupt and discredited "calamity department" was replaced by a slimmed-down and modernized National Institute for the Management of Emergencies.

These children, now grown, still talk about calamidades, except that in urban Maputo, the colourful word has taken on a slightly new meaning.

With $100 a month, a Mozambican need not be too con-

---

[7] William Finnegan, *A Complicated War: The Harrowing of Mozambique* (Berkeley: University of California Press, 1992).

cerned about where his or her next meal is coming from. That level of income even leaves a little extra to spend at the local used clothing stores, shopping for calamidades, the word now used to describe the boatloads of used clothing donated by wealthy nations and sold in poor ones.

Timóteo showed me his shoulder bag, a stylish grey bag with the initials DKNY branded on its top. It is in good condition, which also means that it was not cheap. Calamidades, Timóteo said, are becoming very expensive. He spoke as if they have a cool allure about them, not unlike, I suppose, teenagers at home who shop at the local Value Village in search of the prized bowling shirt or hardware store uniform with some stranger's name embroidered on the breast pocket.

He pointed at the running shoes on my feet. Another example of something that he could buy at the local calamity shop, he said.

For those living in the city, Mozambique has taken a small step back from the precipice of poverty. Enough of a step back that these children have now grown up and purchase their calamidades at local shops rather than waiting for them to arrive by air drop.

A tentative step, but a hopeful one.

In urban Mozambique, calamity has become a good thing.

All Mixed Up

It is incredibly unfair for you to impose yourselves on a village where you are so linguistically deaf and dumb that you do not even understand what you are doing, or what people think of you (Ivan Illich, "To Hell With Good Intentions" Speech, 1968).

When we first arrived in Mozambique, we sat at a restaurant and did our best pointing job to order a great meal. When it came time for dessert, Laura asked the waiter to describe the ice cream dish (a bold move, given the few words of Portuguese we could understand at the time). He said that it contained maça. Apple. Sounds good, Laura thought, and ordered it.

Except that he did not say maça. He said massa. Spaghetti.

Strange. Even stranger that spaghetti-infused ice cream is on the menu at all. We have seen it at several restaurants since, though we have not been able to find a single Mozambican who confesses to eating the stuff.

Not long after Laura's spaghetti incident, I was helping out at the seminary construction project. Geraldo asked me for some massa. This time, I was on the ball. I knew he did not want an apple. But did he want me to buy him a plate of spaghetti?

Turns out that massa—which literally means "mixture"—is also mortar for bricks.

For better or for worse, I will never know all the mistakes that I have made trying to speak Portuguese. Once in a while the confusion is unearthed and corrected. One of the most memorable occasions happened while having a conversation with Jeronimo, a non-Christian. Wanting to learn more about me, he asked a simple question: "Why is it that you are a missionary but do not attend church?"

"I do not attend church?" I asked, confused. Why would he have that impression?

"You told me a couple of weeks ago that you do not attend church."

Why would I tell him that? Surely I did not. Or maybe I had meant to tell him that I did not attend church one particular Sunday?

As simple as that, an innocuous (though significant) misunderstanding takes root, merely because I apparently used the wrong verb tense in a long-forgotten conversation.

Potholes, Padlocks and Poverty

Ivan Illich was a combative social thinker who was infamous for his biting critiques of missionaries and other "dogooders...pretentiously imposing" ourselves on foreign cultures. His critiques are most painful when he succeeds at digging his teeth a little too close to the truth. The truth is, Laura and I have often felt linguistically deaf and dumb this year. The truth is, our lack of fluency has stunted the growth of our relationships both in depth and breadth.

Language is a barrier that has prevented us from getting to know more than a handful of Mozambicans really well.

Unlike Mr. Illich, I do not think that linguistic and cultural barriers are insurmountable. I do not think that missionaries are necessarily living in their adopted countries as invasive salesmen and unwelcome propagators of Western culture.

Some are, sure. But not all. I have witnessed some good examples of "my-way-or-the-highway" theology, but I have also witnessed some better examples of people who love the sick, who love the forgotten, who love the poor. People who spend their time learning about their Mozambican neighbours, sharing meals with them and tears with them, learning from them, and only when necessary, teaching them. People like Ann, a nurse, who helped a mother through toxaemia and taught her to feed her premature child when the hospital could not provide adequate care.

We cannot love our neighbours without knowing our neighbours, and we cannot know our neighbours without learning to talk to them. But the very act of learning their language builds bonds of trust.

Yes, it is difficult. Yes, it takes time. Yes, we will look foolish at times. We might even bring construction workers a surprise (but welcomed) plate of spaghetti once or twice. If that is the price of friendship, let me look foolish.

NOW, UNLOCK YOUR OWN MISSION FIELD

1. What beliefs do you hold to unwaveringly? Are there reasons for holding tightly to these beliefs? Why might other Christians hold different beliefs or challenge your own beliefs?
2. Ivan Illich contests that there is harm in exporting our culture to other areas of the world. What Christian beliefs do you hold that are based in scripture? Which are based in your traditions or culture? Can we accomplish the Great Commission without exporting our culture? Why or why not?

Challenge Yourself:

Identify a poor community near your home, and spend some time walking its streets and observing its people. What is the differential diagnosis for their poverty? What makes them poor? Why are they poor? How can their lives be improved? Do they want your help?

12 A Prayer for Africa

Once Again, An Empty Home

Despite constant change, life has a way of going in circles. There is a first time for everything, but even many of these firsts feel strangely familiar. We are back at one of those moments today. Back at the beginning of the circle.

Furniture has been moved out of our apartment, sold in order to fill a deficit in our fundraising account. Laura and I are living amidst barely more than a few stray dust balls recently exposed to the light of day.

For Laura, school finished this week. We are standing in the wake of an exodus of foreigners: diplomats returning home for summer vacations, business men and women returning to head offices, missionaries going home to raise more money.

Our stomachs are overflowing with the bounty of farewell dinners, some hosted by us, some held in our honour. We are sad to leave behind so many people we did not even know a year ago. Many people have asked us about plans to return, but we offer no promises. Perhaps we will meet again. Perhaps only in heaven.

We have been eager to finish well, eager to maintain motivation and energy right up to our departing moments, but our minds are drifting back home. It has been difficult to kindle new friendships that we know will be difficult to sustain in such a short time.

And we are only too aware that, for the Mozambicans that we leave behind, their stories started long before we arrived and will extend far into the future. We will soon be forgotten by all but our closest friends, replaced in body and memory by a new set of missionaries with different perspectives, different backgrounds, different ways of doing things. Perhaps missionaries from North America; perhaps missionaries from Africa.

We are ready to return home, though not entirely ready to leave this home. And we realize that the home we return to will not be the home we left a year ago—not because it has changed, but because we have changed. Because we have spent the past year being transformed in the crucible of God's hands.

We have been living a life that, despite our best efforts, slide presentations and photographs will never completely convey. Our friends and family will never completely be able to relate to the stories we share. And our friends and family have continued to live their lives over the past year as well. Their own stories have continued on, and we are all faced with the task of weaving these two divergent stories back together.

In just a few days we will experience another shock as we once again splash the crisp, cool water of our home culture on our faces. And have the freedom once again to brush our teeth with the convenience of tap water.

Jesus Christ is the same yesterday and today and forever. And He is the same in Mozambique as in North America as everywhere. His constancy is the foundation that will keep us anchored as we prepare for yet another transition.

Quiet Confidence

Reflecting on today's departure from Mozambique adds a certain depth of understanding to a much more significant departure that took place some 2,000 years ago. Imagine the contrast that an honestly reflective Jesus would have seen: the gulf between His perfect self and the young, imperfect church that He created.

Jesus' ministry lasted all of three years. Three years to identify, train, and mentor a small band of misfit fishermen and tax collectors to share an incredible story of salvation with an unbelieving people. Three years to build the ultimate in self-sustaining and self-propagating ministries.

Imagine the disciples' fears as Jesus began to foretell His departure: "We are not ready for you to leave us," they surely would have complained. "Can we please go over those parables once more, just to make sure that we understand them?"

"Jesus, can you please edit this early manuscript of the gospels? If you do not have time to read them completely, at least read the red-ink parts, just to make sure we have captured Your words properly."

Their fears ran deep, and they were well-founded. Even the rock upon which Jesus chose to build the church, His disciple Peter, was woefully and completely unprepared. Peter's disappointing last act with Jesus involved drawing his sword in a fit of uncontrolled anger and chopping off the ear of the servant of the high priest who was arresting Jesus.

This is the rock upon which God will build His church.

Shortly afterwards, as Jesus is facing His day in court and the crucifixion plan is irreversibly set into motion, Peter denies knowing Jesus. He denies being a disciple of the Most High God to none other than an unthreatening, harmless little girl standing in a doorway. "But I am not ready to assume responsibility as the rock," Peter must have protested to Jesus.

Jesus had predicted Peter's failures and yet chose to follow through with the plans of the Father, despite the protestations of those who followed Him.

In fact, the only disciple pleased about God's timetable might have been Judas Iscariot, eager to receive his 30 silver coins for having betrayed our Saviour.

And yet God did not revise His schedule. He did not delay the crucifixion just a couple more weeks to make sure that everyone was prepared for His Son's departure.

Jesus knew that it was time for Him to go and had a quiet confidence that, in His short ministry, He had set the wheels in motion for the world to hear His wonderful story—and knew that, without His departure, the disciples would forever remain pupils, never making the leap to teachers and fishers of men. He left, trusting His disciples to make mistakes, to learn, and to stumble through. And today, 2,000 years later, their legacy remains: a large yet imperfect church that worships a most perfect God.

Jesus' own ministry was no less than the salvation of the world, and He had the confidence to leave it in the hands of a flock of flawed followers. Learning from His example, I too can have the confidence to leave the ministry that I have worked to build over the past year in the hands of Mario and Samuel. Its success is far from assured, but they will struggle to take it in the direction that they see best for Mozambique.

So here you are, Mario and Samuel, I hand this program off from one cracked pot to another. My airplane awaits.

Now, Unlock Your Own Mission Field

1. What transitions are you facing right now in your life? What activities are helpful for managing this transition? What activities might be harmful?
2. The institution of the church was created and is sustained by fallible humans—people like you and me. In what ways is the institution helpful? In what ways can it be improved? How have your

experiences with the institution of church shaped your experience with God?

Challenge Yourself:

Select a country that has been in the news recently: front page news, the kind that would discourage you from travelling there. Perhaps Afghanistan or Iraq. Maybe Zimbabwe or Somalia. Find out what you can about that country using as many varied sources as possible. Go to a travel agent and find tourist brochures that highlight the beauty of that country. Go to a library or internet café and see what you can learn about life in those countries between the punctuations of tragedy. Commit to praying continually for that country and its people.

Bibliography

Finnegan, William. *A Complicated War: The Harrowing of Mozambique.* Berkeley: University of California Press, 1992.

Maranz, David E. *African Friends and Money Matters: Observations from Africa* (Publications in Ethnography, Vol. 37). SIL International, 2001.

Myers, Bryant. *Walking With the Poor: Principles and Practices of Transformational Development.* New York: Orbis Books, 1999.

Posterski, Donald C. *Enemies With Smiling Faces: Defeating the Subtle Threats that Endanger Christians.* Illinois: InterVarsity Press, 2004.

Sachs, Jeffrey D. *The End of Poverty: Economic Possibilities for Our Time.* New York: Penguin Group, 2006.

Smith, Ian Douglas. *The Great Betrayal: The Memoirs of Ian Douglas Smith.* London: Blake Publishing, 1997.

Yunus, Muhammad. *Banker to the Poor: Micro-lending and the Battle Against World Poverty.* New York: Public Affairs, 2003.

Nov 8/07

Visit us online at
www.StevenMKuhn.com